The Oxford India Anthology of

TWELVE MODERN INDIAN POETS

The Oxford India Anthology of

TWELVE MODERN
INDIAN POETS

Chosen and Edited by
ARVIND KRISHNA MEHROTRA

DELHI
OXFORD UNIVERSITY PRESS
BOMBAY CALCUTTA MADRAS
1992

Oxford University Press, Walton Street, Oxford OX2 6DP

NEW YORK TORONTO
DELHI BOMBAY CALCUTTA MADRAS KARACHI
PETALING JAYA SINGAPORE HONG KONG TOKYO
NAIROBI DAR ES SALAAM
MELBOURNE AUCKLAND

AND ASSOCIATES IN
BERLIN IBADAN

SBN 0 19 562867/5

Printed in India by P. K. Ghosh
at Eastend Printers, 3 Dr Suresh Sarkar Road, Calcutta 700 014
and published by S. K. Mookerjee, Oxford University Press
YMCA Library Building, Jai Singh Road, New Delhi 110 001

In memory of

AMIT RAI

31 May 1948, Jabalpur
21 June 1966, Bombay

Contents

CONTENTS

CONTENTS

CONTENTS

Contents

Preface

I could not have edited this anthology without the co-operation of its poets. They sent me such books of theirs as I did not possess, and made available their scattered prose writings and interviews: my files are thick with newspaper clippings, offprints, photocopies. These became the basis of the introductory notes in which, as far as possible, I try and describe the work of each poet in his own words. The criticism of Indian poetry in English that has come out of our universities' English Departments is both voluminous and of inferior quality, and is best left alone.

The footnotes and select bibliography, however, do not indicate some other debts: to Madhusudan Prasad, for the loan of two books; to Vandana, my wife, for her patience; to my editors and printer for their editorial care; and to Sara Rai and Smita Agarwal for offering help when I needed it most.

ARVIND KRISHNA MEHROTRA

Allahabad, 1 February 1992

Acknowledgements

The editor and publishers gratefully acknowledge permission to reproduce copyright poems in this book.

NISSIM EZEKIEL

For 'A Poem of Dedication', 'My Cat', 'For Love's Record', 'Case Study', 'Poet, Lover, Birdwatcher', 'Paradise Flycatcher', 'Two Images' and 'After Reading a Prediction' from *Collected Poems*, published by Oxford University Press, to the author and the publishers.

JAYANTA MAHAPATRA

For 'A Rain of Rites', 'Hunger', 'The Moon Moments', 'The Abandoned British Cemetery at Balasore', 'The Captive Air of Chandipur-on-Sea' and 'The Vase' from *Selected Poems*, published by Oxford University Press, to the author and the publishers. For 'I Hear My Fingers Sadly Touching an Ivory Key' and 'Hands' from *A Rain of Rites*, published from the University of Georgia Press, to the author and the publishers. For 'A Kind of Happiness' and 'The Door' from *The False Start*, published by Clearing House, to the author and the publishers. For 'Of that Love' from *Life Signs*, published by Oxford University Press, to the author and the publishers. For 'Days' and 'Waiting' from *Burden of Waves and Fruit*, published by Three Continents Press, to the author and the publishers.

A. K. RAMANUJAN

For 'The Striders', 'Breaded Fish', 'Looking for a Cousin on a Swing', 'Self-Portrait', 'Anxiety' and 'Case History' from *The Striders*, published by Oxford University Press, to the author and the publishers. For 'Love Poem for a Wife. 2' and 'The Hindoo: the Only Risk' from *Relations*, published by Oxford University Press, to the author and the publishers. For 'Snakes and Ladders', 'On the Death of a Poem', 'Highway Stripper', 'Moulting' and 'Chicago Zen' from *Second Sight*, published by Oxford University Press, to the author and the publishers.

xv

ARUN KOLATKAR

For 'Woman', 'Suicide of Rama' and 'Irani Restaurant Bombay' from *An Anthology of Marathi Poetry: 1945–1965*, published by Nirmala Sadanand, to the author and the publishers. For 'Crabs' and 'Biograph' from *Ekādash*, published by Bharat Bhavan, to the author and Bharat Bhavan, Bhopal. For 'The Bus', 'Heart of Ruin', 'Chaitanya', 'A Low Temple', 'The Pattern', 'The Horseshoe Shrine', 'Manohar', 'Chaitanya', 'The Butterfly', 'A Scratch', 'Ajamil and the Tigers', 'Chaitanya', 'Between Jejuri and the Railway Station' and 'The Railway Station' from *Jejuri*, published by Clearing House, to the author and the publishers.

KEKI N. DARUWALLA

For 'Hawk', 'The King Speaks to the Scribe' and 'The Unrest of Desire' from *The Keeper of the Dead*, published by Oxford University Press, to the author and the publishers. For 'Wolf', 'Fish are Speared by Night', 'Chinar' and 'Night Fishing' from *Landscapes*, published by Oxford University Press, to the author and the publishers.

DOM MORAES

For 'Autobiography', 'Words to a Boy', 'Two from Israel', 'Prophet', 'Key', 'Interludes VII' and 'Sinbad' from *Collected Poems 1957–1987*, published by Penguin Books, to the author and the publishers. For 'Steles I, IV, VI, VII, VIII, X' and 'Future Plans' from *Serendip*, published by Viking, to the author and the publishers.

DILIP CHITRE

For 'The Light of Birds Breaks the Lunatic's Sleep' from *An Anthology of Marathi Poetry: 1945–1965*, published by Nirmala Sadanand, to the author and the publishers. For 'Travelling in a Cage 2, 5, 7, 8, 19, 21', 'In Limbo', 'Pushing a Cart', 'Of Garlic and Such', 'The Felling of the Banyan Tree', 'Father Returning Home' and 'Panhala' from *Travelling in a Cage*, published by Clearing House, to the author and the publishers.

EUNICE DE SOUZA

For 'Feeding the Poor at Christmas', 'Sweet Sixteen', 'Miss Louise', 'Forgive Me, Mother', 'For My Father, Dead Young' and 'de Souza

Prabhu' from *Fix*, published by Newground, to the author and the publishers. For 'Women in Dutch Painting', 'She and I', 'Eunice', 'Advice to Women', 'For Rita's Daughter, Just Born' and 'Five London Pieces III', from *Women in Dutch Painting*, published by Praxis, to the author and the publishers.

ADIL JUSSAWALLA

For 'Land's End', 'Evening on a Mountain', 'Halt X' and 'Bats' from *Land's End*, published by Writers Workshop, to the author and the publishers. For 'Missing Person 1.3, 1.6, 1.7, 1.9, 1.13, II.1, II.2, II.5', 'Nine Poems on Arrival' and 'Freedom Song' from *Missing Person*, published by Clearing House, to the author and the publishers. For 'Connection' to the author and *Bombay Literary Review*.

AGHA SHAHID ALI

For 'Postcard from Kashmir', 'Snowmen', 'Cracked Portraits', 'The Dacca Gauzes', 'The Season of the Plains' and 'The Previous Occupant' from *The Half-Inch Himalayas*, published by Wesleyan University Press, to the author and the publishers.

VIKRAM SETH

For 'Guest' from *Mappings*, published by Writers Workshop, to the author and the publishers. For 'The Humble Administrator's Garden', 'Evening Wheat', 'The Accountant's House', 'From an "East is Red" Steamer', 'Ceasing Upon the Midnight' and 'Unclaimed' from *The Humble Administrator's Garden*, published by Oxford University Press, to the author and the publishers. For lines from *The Golden Gate*, published by Faber and Faber, to the author and the publishers. For 'Soon' from *All You Who Sleep Tonight*, published by Viking, to the author and the publishers.

MANOHAR SHETTY

For 'Fireflies', 'Foreshadows' and 'Gifts' from *A Guarded Space*, published by Newground, to the author and the publishers. For 'Wounds', 'Domestic Creatures', 'Bats' and 'Departures' from *Borrowed Time*, published by Praxis, to the author and the publishers. For 'Moving Out' to the author and *Bombay Literary Review*.

Introduction

For the purposes of the Introduction I recently reread an old essay of mine, and while it was no surprise to find how little my views had changed in the ten years since it was written, one paragraph did make me wince.[1] In it I said that anthologies are graveyards, and the anthologist's job is to see only the best corpses get in. I also called the title of one selection 'misleading and cocky' because it failed to indicate that the choice of Indian poets was restricted to those who write in English. I now wish I had found a less deathly metaphor for anthologies and their compilers, and not dwelt on the misleading title at all.

Indians have been writing verse in English at least since the 1820s and it goes under many ludicrous names—Indo-English, India-English, Indian English, Indo-Anglian, and even Anglo-Indian and Indo-Anglican. 'Kill that nonsense term', Adil Jussawalla said of Indo-Anglian, 'and kill it quickly.' The term may not be easy to destroy, but much of the poetry it describes, especially that written between 1825 and 1945, is truly dead. Later poets have found no use for it, and a literary tradition is of no use to anyone else.

The origins of modern Indian poetry in English go no further back than the poets in this anthology. But it would have been different, I think, if one poet in particular had shown as much talent as she did hospitality. Consider the following passage in Noel Stock's *Life of Ezra Pound* (1970):

> During the second half of 1913, at the home in London of the Bengali poetess, Sarojini Naidu, Pound met an American widow, Mrs Mary Fenollosa. After reading Pound's 'Contemporania' and possibly other poems Mrs Fenollosa decided that he was the one to whom she could entrust the literary remains of her late husband Ernest Fenollosa.

How Pound famously transformed the Fenollosa notebooks into

[1] 'The Emperor Has No Clothes', *Chandrabhāgā* (Cuttack), No. 3 (Summer 1980), 17–22, and No. 7 (Summer 1982), 1–32.

Cathay does not concern us here. My interest in the record of that day in 1913 is to point out the opportunity missed, for among the poems in 'Contemporania' were some of the finest examples of Imagist verse:

> Like a skein of loose thread blown against a wall
> She walks by the railing of a path in Kensington
> Gardens . . .
>
> ('The Garden')

Unfortunately Mrs Naidu never looked beyond the social fringes of modernism, and whereas the new movement would have benefited her work, she, undistracted by it, continued to write as before, as though nothing had changed. However, one doesn't like being unkind to her. She knew her limitations only too well, once saying in a letter to Arthur Symons, 'I am not a poet really. I have the vision and the desire, but not the voice.'[2] Her last book was published in 1917 and thereafter, displaying a fine sense of judgement, she wrote little poetry. The same, though, cannot be said of Aurobindo Ghose, who spent the last years of his life composing a worthless epic of 24,000 lines.

II

'I make a pact with you, Walt Whitman—'

—Ezra Pound

Henry Derozio, Toru Dutt, Aurobindo Ghose, and Sarojini Naidu were courageous and perhaps charming men and women, but not those with whom you could today do business. The poets of the post-Independence period had therefore to make their pacts elsewhere. Some were made in their own backyard (with Kapilar, Paranar, Basavanna, Allama Prabhu, Kabir, Tukaram, Nirala, Faiz), and some overseas (with Browning, Yeats, Eliot, Pound, Auden, Williams, Stevens, Lowell, Ginsberg). The enterprise involved certain risks. As Adil Jussawalla's 'two-bit hero' Missing Person—a projection of the third world bourgeois intellectual—realizes in the course of his short but violent life, the transactions with others, the transformations of the self, do not always go off smoothly:

[2] Quoted in K. R. Ramachandran Nair, *Three Indo-Anglian Poets: Henry Derozio, Toru Dutt and Sarojini Naidu*, New Delhi, Sterling, 1983, 93.

> What bit-parts, what a fall
> for one we thought had gone
> proud to adventure—
>
> ('Missing Person', II.6)

In Jussawalla's sequence, a missing person is not just what our hero becomes, it's what he is, his very condition defined by absence, 'the central absence of the Indo-Anglian psyche'.[3] Taking the prospect from a different angle, or maybe it's a different prospect, A. K. Ramanujan, Arun Kolatkar, and Agha Shahid Ali see there a varied presence. Ramanujan darkly juggles with his selves, slipping into one and out the other, keeping several going at the same time. A statement of his is often quoted:

> English and my disciplines (linguistics, anthropology) give me my 'outer' forms—linguistic, metrical, logical and other such ways of shaping experience; and my first thirty years in India, my frequent visits and fieldtrips, my personal and professional pre-occupations with Kannada, Tamil, the classics and folklore give me my substance, my 'inner' forms, images and symbols. They are continuous with each other, and I no longer can tell what comes from where.[4]

A poem by Arun Kolatkar is a pattern cut in language, the grainy material without which there would be no self to speak of. What name we afterwards give the material makes little difference:

> मै भाभीको बोला
> क्या भाईसाबके ड्यूटीपे मै आ जाऊ ?
> भडक गयी साली
> रहमान बोला गोली चलाउ'गा
> मै बोला एक रंडीके वास्ते ?
> चलाव गोली गांडू

The poem is written in Bombay Hindi, published in Kolatkar's book of Marathi poems, translated by him into American English, and,

[3] Homi Bhabha, 'Indo-Anglian Attitudes', *Times Literary Supplement*, 3 February 1978, 136.

[4] Quoted in *Ten Twentieth-Century Indian Poets*, ed. R. Parthasarathy, Delhi, 1976, 95.

3

rightly, has been included in an anthology of Indian verse in English:

allow me beautiful
i said to my sister in law
to step in my brother's booties
you had it coming said rehman
a gun in his hand
shoot me punk
kill your brother i said
for a bloody cunt

('Three Cups of Tea')[5]

'Three Cups of Tea' suggests the idea that all languages are perhaps one language. It also makes you ask if language is not in the end superfluous to poetry. Kolatkar himself appears to believe it is so, for in matters linguistic he is a monk, renouncing all but the most essential words, keeping punctuation to a minimum, and shunning the excitement of the first person singular.

Making a statement on his work, Agha Shahid Ali spoke for many of his contemporaries when he said,

I think we in the subcontinent have been granted a rather unique opportunity: to contribute to the English language in ways that the British, the Americans, and the Australians, also the Canadians, cannot. We can do things with the syntax that will bring the language alive in rich and strange ways, and though poetry should have led the way, it is a novelist, Salman Rushdie, who has shown the poets *a* way: he has, to quote an essay I read somewhere, chutnified English. And the confidence to do this could only have come in the post-Independence generation. The earlier generations followed the rules inflicted by the rulers so strictly that it is almost embarrassing. They also followed models, especially the models of realism, in ways that imprisoned them. I think we can do a lot more. What I am looking forward to—to borrow another metaphor from food—is the biryanization (I'm chutnifying) of English. Behind my work, I hope, readers can sometimes hear the music of Urdu. Of course, all this has to do with an emotional identification on my part with north Indian Muslim culture, which is steeped in Urdu. I, as I have grown older, have felt the need to identify myself as a north Indian Muslim (not in any sectarian sense but in a cultural sense). And I do not feel that this culture is necessarily the

[5] *Contemporary Indian Poetry in English: An Assessment and Selection*, ed. Saleem Peeradina, Bombay, 1972, 44.

4

province of the Muslims (after all, Firaq Gorakhpuri was a Hindu) and many non-Muslim Indians can also consider themselves culturally Muslim. I am not familiar with Saleem Peeradina's work, but I think I am among the very few of the Indians writing in English who is identifying himself in these terms. However, I do not want in all cases to be straitjacketed by these remarks; I want this to be a prominent but not exclusive element in my work.[6]

Ali's metaphors from north Indian cuisine seem a long way off indeed from R. Parthasarathy's cry, 'My tongue in English chains'.

III

With important exceptions, which in the present selection are the poems of Dom Moraes and Vikram Seth and the early poems of Adil Jussawalla, the native tongue, whether as Ramanujan's 'inner' form, Kolatkar's parallel text, or Ali's 'music of Urdu', operates behind the English lines of several poets. However, we still know very little about the subject, and can make only conjectural models to show the organization and interplay of languages in multilingual sensibilities. According to one rather crude model, languages in the polyglot's brain are arranged in layers, one above the other: the language we licked off our mothers' teats in the first, those picked up from the neighbours in the second, and English, the language learnt at school—and the language that will happen for the rest of our lives, bright as a butterfly's wing or a piece of tin aimed at the throat, to paraphrase from Jussawalla's 'Missing Person'—in the topmost layer. A problem with this model is that it treats the Indian poet as someone who chiefly transports linguistic and cultural materials from the bottom to the surface, from Indian mother tongue to English, which is all very well except that it tends to narrowly equate Indian poetry with Indianness. A good poem is a good poem, and not because it matches the colour of the poet's skin or passport.

What Parthasarathy wrote in Ramanujan's defence following the publication of an article mildly critical of him in Jayanta Mahapatra's magazine, *Chandrabhāgā*, is one example of the limiting view of poetry that follows on the 'layer' model. 'It seems to me', said Parthasarathy,

> that Ramanujan's work offers the first indisputable evidence of the *validity* of Indian English verse. Both *The Striders* (1966) and

[6] Letter to the editor from Agha Shahid Ali, 1988.

Relations (1971) are the heir of an anterior tradition, a tradition very much of this subcontinent, the deposits of which are in Kannada and Tamil, and which have been assimilated into English. Ramanujan's deepest roots are in the Tamil and Kannada past, and he has repossessed that past, in fact made it available in the English language. I consider this a *significant* achievement . . . 'Prayers to Lord Murugan' is, for instance, embedded in, and arises from, a specific tradition. It is, in effect, the first step towards establishing an indigenous tradition of Indian English verse.[7]

By saying that 'Prayers to Lord Murugan' is embedded in another tradition which Ramanujan makes available to us, Parthasarathy is already reducing languages which are tissued in the multilingual sensibility to pictural shreds, to the framed surfaces of oleographs. The other tradition does not enter a poem by Ramanujan, Kolatkar, or Ali in the guise of god, a river, a place, a cow named Gopi, or a Tipu Sultan; nor as a poetic shell, a *rubai*, *dohā*, *vacana*, or *abhanga*. Ramanujan himself is ambiguous about the points at which native idiom interferes with English: 'I no longer can tell what comes from where.' Instead of assigning languages fixed positions in a hierarchical system, he sees them as territories with soft borders across which movement is unrestricted, and not just for literary forms and colourful gods, and not only in one direction. The movement is in his case from Kannada and Tamil into English and, as importantly, from English into Kannada. The languages Ramanujan writes in, those he translates from, and those he translates into are 'continuous with each other'.

Each poet's 'continuous' language or idiolect is constituted differently: Ramanujan's is of English-Kannada-Tamil, Kolatkar's and Chitre's of English-Marathi, Ali's of English-Urdu, Mahapatra's of English-Oriya, and Jussawalla has in an interview spoken of 'various languages crawling around inside [his] head'.[8] The continuity may not always be with another Indian language. Eunice de Souza makes hers continuous with a variety of English itself, a pidgin spoken only in the suburbs of Bombay.

> Che bugger Pitu sas
> asli chick men

is from an unpublished group of her poems titled 'Queen's English'.

[7] 'Letters', *Chandrabhāgā* (Cuttack), No. 2 (Winter 1979), 66.

[8] Peter Nazareth, 'Adil Jussawalla Interviewed', *Vāgartha* (New Delhi), No. 25 (April 1979), 5.

Ramanujan's 'Chicago Zen' treats of the multilingual poet's two-fold condition, his interior spaces divided on the one hand and conjoined on the other, and the mishaps, the falls and descents, that attend his—a missing person's—revelations:

> Watch your step. Sight may strike you
> blind in unexpected places.
>
> The traffic light turns orange
> on 57th and Dorchester, and you stumble,
>
> you fall into a vision of forest fires,
> enter a frothing Himalayan river,
>
> rapid, silent.

IV

Even after two hundred years, the Indian poet who writes in English is looked upon with suspicion by other Indian writers, as though he did not belong either to the subcontinent of his birth or its literature. The romantic idea that poetic expression is possible only in the mother tongue has led to several misconceptions about him, one of which is that he writes for a foreign audience, and his readers are not in Allahabad and Cuttack but Boston and London. An editorial in *Frontier*, a left-wing weekly of Calcutta, recently said:

> And it is not just a tryst with freak destiny that present-day Indian poets writing in English, such as Gieve Patel, A. K. Ramanujan, R. Parthasarathy, P. Lal, Vikram Seth, Adil Jussawalla, Keshav Malik and Keki Daruwalla, who are well-known to Western countries and hog up literature columns in English dailies spewed out of Indian mega cities, are treated as irrelevant by the vernacular academicians due to absence of nativity.[9]

The delirious statement is not worthy even of denial. However, I should still like to think that provincial ignorance rather than intellectual hatred causes it, for though many have heard the names of these Indian poets, few have read them, and even fewer know anything about the size and extent of the readership. For instance, how many would know that during the seventies and eighties several important

[9] 'Indian Poetry in English', *Frontier* (Calcutta), 26 May 1990, 1.

collections of verse came out from small presses? The books included Jayanta Mahapatra's *The False Start* (1980), Arun Kolatkar's *Jejuri* (1976), Dilip Chitre's *Travelling in a Cage* (1980), Eunice de Souza's *Fix* (1979) and *Women in Dutch Painting* (1988), Adil Jussawalla's *Missing Person* (1976), and Manohar Shetty's *A Guarded Space* (1981) and *Borrowed Time* (1988). The editions were small and the distribution negligible, and some titles are now out of print. It's a situation in which anthologies become necessary. They may not save modern Indian verse in English from being damned, but at least they make parts of it available to those who first wish to read it.

To edit an anthology is an opportunity to revise the literary map, bring neglected works back in circulation, and shift the emphasis from certain poets to others. This has been done by omitting Kamala Das and R. Parthasarathy (my objections to the latter are set out in the essay referred to at the beginning of the Introduction); by including Kolatkar's uncollected early poems and Chitre's sequence 'Travelling in a Cage'; and by giving Ezekiel fewer lines than Mahapatra, Ramanujan, and Kolatkar. I have wanted to reveal through a particular choice of poets and poems the sharp-edged quality of Indian verse. It is not its best-known aspect, and my introductory notes to the poets reflect both the moments when I succeeded in discovering it and those when I was disappointed.

There have been in the past similar anthologies from the post-Independence period—by Saleem Peeradina (1971), R. Parthasarathy (1976), Keki N. Daruwalla (1980), Vilas Sarang (1990), and Kaiser Haq (1990)—but none of them made any difference to the accepted shape of Indian verse in English, and considering what is available in it at present, this is not surprising. On the other hand, there certainly is room for a larger, more comprehensive selection, one that will include poets like Fredoon Kabraji and Beram Saklatvala who are virtually unknown (their books were published by the same vanity press in London that did Ezekiel's first collection), Ruskin Bond and L. P. Bantleman who are always overlooked, and younger poets like Menka Shivdasani, Vijay Nambisan, and Tabish Khair. In fact I have edited this anthology hoping these and other young poets will find something to preserve in what was made by earlier strugglers in the desert.

Nissim Ezekiel

Nissim Ezekiel was born in Bombay in 1924 of Jewish (Bene-Israel) parents, and educated at Wilson College, Bombay, and Birkbeck College, London. After working in journalism, advertising and broadcasting, he took up a teaching job in 1961, and at the time of retirement was Professor of English at the University of Bombay. In addition to eight volumes of poetry—*A Time to Change* (1952), *Sixty Poems* (1953), *The Third* (1958), *The Unfinished Man* (1960), *The Exact Name* (1965), *Hymns in Darkness* (1976), *Latter-Day Psalms* (1982), selected for the Sahitya Akademi Award of 1983, and *Collected Poems* (1989)—Ezekiel has written plays, art criticism, and reviews. He is at present the editor of *The Indian P.E.N.*, and has in the past edited *Quest*, *Imprint* and *Poetry India*. He was awarded the Padma Shri in 1988.

My own appreciation of Ezekiel's poetry has been slow in coming, and even now I cannot always read it without reservation. Often the writing seems purposeless ('At twenty-seven or so / I met the girl who's now / my wife. As bride and groom / we went for what is usually called— / I don't know why—a honeymoon.'); the language under no pressure ('You arrived / with sari clinging / to your breast / and hips.'); and if one may shift the poetic reference from context to author, the man himself hopelessly priapic (' "Is this part of you?" she asks, / as she holds it, stares at it. / Then she laughs.').

Quite apart from being the first modern poet in the literature, Ezekiel was himself a good poet once. He possessed a quick observant eye and could encompass a life in the space of a line, as when he says of an old woman, 'She lived on cornflakes, hate and sweetened milk'. His first book is called *A Time to Change*, and Ezekiel could not have been unaware of the aptness of the title. In the absence of a good literary history, it is difficult to say what sustained this heir to Sarojini Naidu's mellifluous drivel when he started out as a young poet in the mid-forties. The espousal of the self in his work is perhaps one consequence of the realization that he must create his own life-support system. There was nothing in the literature then, or even in the following decade, that could have sustained him. As 'History' puts

9

it, 'It all comes back to individual man / And what he chooses'. In this case the 'individual man' chose to 'dream of angels', and did so in English at a time when the dream and its chosen language had few backers.

Writing towards the end of *Collected Poems*, Ezekiel describes himself as

> . . . a drug-addict
> whose drugs are work, sensuality,
> poetry, and the dance of the self . . .
>
> ('A Different Way')

If self-preoccupation is stamped on the obverse of his coin, the figure of a healer is on the reverse. In the very next poem, the title, 'At 62', making its concluding lines even more plangent, he says

> I want my hands
> to learn how to heal
> myself and others,
> before I hear
> my last song.

The conflict between the opposing images on the coin arose but seldom. The desire to heal others presupposes an openness to the world outside the self, and Ezekiel's poetry—though now and then it admits a wide-angle view of Bombay ('Barbaric city sick with slums, / Deprived of seasons, blessed with rains'), a city which, one must add, fares better than London ('The London seasons passed me by')—owes no allegiance whatsoever to person, place and thing. On his own admission, 'I close my eyes to see with better sight.' The line is from one of his finest poems:

> There is a landscape certainly, the sea
> Among its broad realities, attracts
> Because it is the symbol of the free
> Demoniac life within,
> Hardly suggested by the surface facts . . .
>
> ('A Poem of Dedication')

When a thing is its symbol and 'facts' are suspect—as if mischievously put there, like wrong fingerposts, to misguide him—who can blame the poet who has made subjectivity his song for taking the precaution of shutting his eyes? The conclusion, which an eighteenth-century

Humanist could not fault, therefore comes as a surprise:

> I want a human balance humanly
> Acquired, fruitful in the common hour.

Taken as a whole, the poem's effect is quite different and doesn't come from its thing-versus-symbol, flux-versus-fixity, a-time-to-act-versus-a-time-to-contemplate argument; it comes, rather, from a third—and spellbound—time. The 'human balance' Ezekiel seeks is already, fleetingly, in his possession. One summer night in June 1933, W. H. Auden experienced something which decades later he characterized as 'The Vision of Agape'. It is to know 'exactly . . . what it means to love one's neighbour as oneself'. Ezekiel's lines are less categorical, but then, being lines of verse, they're the making of the vision itself.

Ezekiel described his second book, *Sixty Poems*, as a 'modest, interim collection'. 'It does not claim to be poetry', he wrote in the Foreword, 'but it reveals a few small discoveries in the pursuit of poetry. That the pursuit is a failure is obvious.'[1] Recent reviewers of Ezekiel make the same point by giving him a 'long and arduous apprenticeship' (Vilas Sarang). Ezekiel's strongest work is undeniably in *The Unfinished Man* and *The Exact Name*, but at the same time his three early volumes are of more than historical interest. 'A Poem of Dedication' is, after all, from *Sixty Poems*, and what needs emphasis is that the two Ezekiels, one compulsively writing bad verse and the other sometimes a good poem, have been around from the beginning. Latterly, though, one has seen little of the other Ezekiel.

At twenty-nine, the age at which he published *Sixty Poems*, Ezekiel was a not unambitious poet in the romantic-ideational tradition. As he says, the only reason for publishing the book was he lacked the courage to destroy it.

> There is in each [poem] a line or phrase, an idea or image, which helps me to maintain some sort of continuity in my life. If I could transcend the personal importance of these poems I would not publish them. I am interested in writing poetry, not in making a personal verse record. But poetry is elusive: to write a poem is comparatively easy.[2]

Behind the distinction between poetry and 'personal record' lies

---

[1] *Sixty Poems*, Bombay, n.p., 1953.
[2] Ibid.

Mallarmé's 'sin of seeing the Dream in its ideal nakedness ... the horrible vision of a pure work'.

Written 2500 years ago are Sappho's lines:

> The moon has set, and the Pleiades.
> It is the middle of the night,
> Hour follows hour. I lie alone.
>
> (tr. Guy Davenport)

Imperishable poetry or immediate record? They are both. It may be too early to talk of the imperishability or otherwise of Ezekiel's poetry, but in several of his best poems—one of them, a version of the fatal woman, in fact called 'For Love's Record'—his plain authentic-enough statements take on the authority of verse, and, in a counter-vailing movement, the metronomic line comes under the charge of a speaking voice. (Just how and when personal record becomes poetry is, however, a subject for the gods.)

Unlike A. K. Ramanujan and Jayanta Mahapatra, Ezekiel will be remembered less for the totality of his work than for individual things in it. From the anthologist's point of view, this makes him an easier poet to cull from. The selection below leaves out some of his familiar anthology pieces—the sentimental 'Night of the Scorpion' for instance—in favour of others so far overlooked. To recall 'Poet, Lover, Birdwatcher', I chose those poems where I felt Ezekiel, like the best poets, waited for words and 'never spoke before his spirit moved'. It's a pity he disregarded this insight so often.

A Poem of Dedication

The view from basement rooms is rather small.
A patch or two of green, a bit of sky,
Children heard but never seen, an old wall,
Two trees, a washing line between, windows
With high curtains to block the outward eye;
It seems that nothing changes, nothing grows,
But suddenly the mind is loosed of chains
And purifies itself before the warm
Mediterranean, which fills the veins,
To make the body beautiful and light—
Heaviness of limbs or soul can mimic calm—
I close the eyes to see with better sight.

There is a landscape certainly, the sea
Among its broad realities, attracts
Because it is a symbol of the free
Demoniac life within,
Hardly suggested by the surface facts,
And rivers what a man can hope to win
By simple flowing, learning how to flow,
And trees imply an obvious need of roots,
Besides that all organic growth is slow.
Both poetry and living illustrate:
Each season brings its own peculiar fruits,
A time to act, a time to contemplate.

The image is created; try to change.
Not to seek release but resolution,
Not to hanker for a wide, god-like range
Of thought, nor the matador's dexterity.
I do not want the yogi's concentration,
I do not want the perfect charity
Of saints nor the tyrant's endless power.
I want a human balance humanly
Acquired, fruitful in the common hour.
This, Elizabeth, is my creation,
Stated in the terms of poetry
I offer it to you in dedication.

My Cat

My cat, unlike Verlaine's or Baudelaire's
Is neither diabolic nor a sphinx.
Though equally at home on laps or chairs,
She will not be caressed, nor plays the minx.

She has a single mood, she's merely bored,
Yawns and walks away, retires to sleep.
Has never sniffed at where the fish is stored
Nor known to relish milk; less cat than sheep.

She does not condescend to chase a rat
Or play with balls of wool or show her claws
To teasing guests, but in my basement flat
Defies all animal and human laws
Of love and hate.

One night I'll drown this cat.

For Love's Record

I watched the woman walk away with him.
And now I think of her as bold and kind,
Who gathered men as shells and put them by.
No matter how they loved she put them by.

I found no evil in her searching eyes.
Such love as hers could bear no common code.
Vibrating woman in her nights of joy,
Who gathered men as shells and put them by.

With her I kept my distance (not too far)
But heard the music of her quickened breath.
Laughing sorceress to harlequins,
Who gathered men as shells and put them by.

Against my will but somewhat reconciled,
I let her go who gave but would not bind.
She grew in love abandoning her ties,
No matter how they loved she put them by.

Case Study

Whatever he had done was not quite right.
The Masters never failed, however weak,
To know when they had sinned against the light.
Can their example purify his sight?
Ought he to practise Yoga, study Greek,
Or bluff his way throughout with brazen cheek?

Beginning with a foolish love affair
After common school and rotten college,
He had the patient will but not the flair
To climb with quick assault the envied stair;
Messed around instead with useless knowledge,
And staked on politics a fatal pledge.

His marriage was the worst mistake of all.
Although he loved his children when they came,
He spoilt them too with just that extra doll,
Or discipline which drove them to the wall.
His wife and changing servants did the same—
A man is damned in that domestic game.

He worked at various jobs and then he stopped
For reasons never clear or quite approved
By those who knew; some almost said he shopped
Around for dreams and projects later dropped
(Though this was quite untrue); he never moved
Unless he found something he might have loved.

He came to me and this is what I said:
'The pattern will remain, unless you break

It with a sudden jerk; but use your head.
Not all returned as heroes who had fled
In wanting both to have and eat the cake.
Not all who fail are counted with the fake.'

Poet, Lover, Birdwatcher

To force the pace and never to be still
Is not the way of those who study birds
Or women. The best poets wait for words.
The hunt is not an exercise of will
But patient love relaxing on a hill
To note the movement of a timid wing;
Until the one who knows that she is loved
No longer waits but risks surrendering—
In this the poet finds his moral proved,
Who never spoke before his spirit moved.

The slow movement seems, somehow, to say much more.
To watch the rarer birds, you have to go
Along deserted lanes and where the rivers flow
In silence near the source, or by a shore
Remote and thorny like the heart's dark floor.
And there the women slowly turn around,
Not only flesh and bone but myths of light
With darkness at the core, and sense is found
By poets lost in crooked, restless flight,
The deaf can hear, the blind recover sight.

Paradise Flycatcher

(An entry in a bird-watcher's diary relates how, while
dozing in his garden, he noticed the long white streamers
of a Paradise Flycatcher moving against the green of a
Casuarina tree. He is delighted for a moment, then re-
members sadly how the previous bird he had seen of the
same species had been shot down while he was admiring
it. This poem is for the bird-watcher, Zafar Futehally.)

White streamers moving briskly on the green
Casuarina, rouse the sleepy watcher
From a dream of rarest birds
To this reality. A grating sound
Is all the language of the bird,
Spelling death to flies and moths
Who go this way to Paradise.
Its mask of black, with tints of green,
Exactly as described in books on Indian birds,
Is legend come alive to the dreamer
Whose eyes are fixed on it in glad surprise.

So many years ago, its predecessor
Came—it was an afternoon like this—
And clung with shaking streamers
To the same Casuarina, catching flies;
But fate that day, not the dreamer only,
Fixed his eyes on it and shot it down.
It lay with red and red upon its white,
Uncommon bird no longer, in the mud.
The live one flashes at the watcher
Chestnut wings; the dead is buried in his mind.

Two Images

I

From the long dark tunnel
of that afternoon, crouching, humped,
waiting for the promised land,
I peeped out like a startled animal
and saw a friend flapping his angelic wings.
I welcomed him.

II

Fish-soul in that silent pool
I found myself supported
by the element I lived in,
but dragged out with the greatest ease
by any fluttering fly
at the end of a hook.

After Reading a Prediction

I am not superstitious,
The Zodiac predicts a new
creative phase of seven years
for Sagittarians. I remind myself
that to be the healer,
not the sick
or the indifferent one
was always my ambition;
and to rage against the barren
not only in friend or stranger
but perfectly familiar
in my own signature.

This is the place
where I was born. I
know it
well. It is home,
which I recognize at last
as a kind of hell
to be made tolerable.
Let the fevers come,
the patterns break
and form again
for me and for the place.
I say to it and to myself:
not to be dead or dying
is a cause for celebration.

Watching spiders climb
the commonplace, ants
co-operate, lakes
reflect the hills of some
remembered holiday,
ships and swans engender
legends, morals, music,
I seek on firmer ground
to improvise my later fiction,
the fallen world
a faithful friend.
I also learn
to make light of the process,
to be the bird in balance
on the turbulent air
and yet as present here
as any solid human body,
heavy, slow and wishbone
breakable, straining to stay young.

Jayanta Mahapatra

Jayanta Mahapatra was born in Cuttack in 1928, and educated locally and at Science College, Patna. For thirty-six years he worked as a physics teacher in different colleges in Orissa and is now retired. 'My origins lie in the lower middle class,' he has said, 'my upbringing was in a narrow rural community; and I learnt English in a missionary school from a British schoolmaster—but mostly from the exciting novels of Ballantyne, Burroughs, and Haggard.'[1] Mahapatra came to poetry at an age when, in his words, 'most poets would have ... shelved their creations in a drawer.'[2] He was thirty-eight years old at the time. His first book of poems, *Close the Sky, Ten by Ten*, appeared in 1971, and it was followed by *Svayamvara and Other Poems* (1971), *A Father's Hours* (1976), *A Rain of Rites* (1976), *Waiting* (1979), *The False Start* (1980), *Life Signs* (1983), *Dispossessed Nests* (1986), *Selected Poems* (1987), *Burden of Waves and Fruit* (1988), and *The Temple* (1989). *Relationship* (1980), a long poem in twelve sections, was selected for the Sahitya Akademi Award of 1981. Mahapatra has also written short stories and essays, and published three volumes of translations from the Oriya. In 1979 he started *Chandrabhāgā*, a literary bi-annual, and was its editor till it ceased publication in 1985, after fourteen issues.

With some few exceptions, Mahapatra's work is a meditation on a single theme: the daily tragedy of having to wake up in a sun-filled room. Apart from everything else, morning, and the intractable things of morning, refuse to participate in what he calls the 'inner world of [the writer's] own making—a world spaced by his own life, of secret allusions, of desire and agony, of the constantly changing alignment between dream and reality.'[3]

If 'the hard forms of day' fill him with moroseness ('I wonder where the day goes. / Even in the bright sun / this was a world I did not know', as one poem wistfully concludes), night has the opposite

[1] 'The Inaudible Resonance in English Poetry in India', *The Literary Criterion* (Mysore), 15, No. 1 (1980), 26–36.
[2] Ibid.
[3] Ibid.

20

effect and makes him chirpy, almost unstoppable.

> Awakening at night, I always return
> to the black world
> beyond the raftered roof and the perfumed bough
> where a lonely moan for justice
> hardens my breath into something
> like the posture of iron.
>
> ('Iron')

When the breath turns to iron, the night sky is the limit, and as every poet knows, this verse-generating gloom fetches great joy. 'Writing a poem [is] a satisfying act,' Mahapatra has said, 'because it helps to bring a happiness, a light to the eyes, a spring to the feet.'[4] From observing her husband at work, Florence Emily Hardy would have recognized the occasion. 'T.H.', she remarked in a letter to Edmund Gosse, '. . . is now, this afternoon writing a poem, with great spirit: always a sign of well-being with him. Needless to say, it is an intensely dismal poem.' But while there are occasional traces of humour in Hardy, I have yet to catch Mahapatra smile.

The essay that describes writing as 'a satisfying act' also calls it 'a rather painful . . . digging out'. In the secretive language he mines, certain words recur whose meaning lies in the body of his work. Thus 'iron' signifies calamity, sometimes personal; 'rain' a past experience that, though painful, is often remembered; 'hands' a woman once loved and unattainable from the start; 'vague' a sudden intake of breath on coming to a vista in his interior landscape; 'door' the unfaceable and inexpressible; 'glass' the innocence of childhood; and 'window' the quotidian world.

These words, furthermore, appear in clusters rather than isolatedly. In 'The Moon Moments', 'vague doors'; in 'Steps in the Dark', 'vague like the opening of a door', through which darkness, voices, feet, water, reeds, and years enter. These or related words occur also in 'A Kind of Happiness', which in addition has the image of a hand kept in a lap. The image is repeated in 'The Moon Moments', though here the hand is not a woman's but his own.

The order of poems in the books is never indeliberate. In *Life Signs*, 'Of that Love' and 'The Vase' appear on facing pages. One

---

[4] 'The Stranger Within: Coming to Terms Through Poetry', *The Dalhousie Review*, 63, No. 3 (1983), 435.

remembers a body loved but not 'lived in'; the other a body more lived in than loved. His best work is a constant reaching out into this conflict.

'Hunger' is one of the few poems that stands, as it were, outside the system. According to Mahapatra,

> The poem is based on a true incident; it could easily have happened to me on the poverty-ridden sands of Gopalpur-on-sea. Often have I imagined myself walking those sands, my solitude and my inherent sexuality working on me, to face the girl inside the dimly-lit palmfrond shack.[5]

The poem unfolds in four dramatic scenes and has even a snatch of conversation. It is, however, spoilt a little towards the end when, in a careless moment, Mahapatra compares the girl's legs to worms.

'Use no superfluous word, no adjective that does not reveal something' is among the first of Ezra Pound's warnings. 'Don't use an expression as "dim lands *of peace*". It dulls the image. It mixes an abstraction with the concrete.' Rather than fall for modernist advice, Mahapatra trusts his own instincts. He is a master of the superfluous word, and is constantly mixing the abstract with the concrete. There is no poet he seems to be touched by, and there is none he is likely to influence. This in itself is an indication of the free-standing universe of his poems.

[5] 'About "Hunger" and Myself', *Keynote* (Bombay), No. 1 (March 1982), 28.

JAYANTA MAHAPATRA

A Rain of Rites

Sometimes a rain comes
slowly across the sky, that turns
upon its grey cloud, breaking away into light
before it reaches its objective.

The rain I have known and traded all this life
is thrown like kelp on the beach.
Like some shape of conscience I cannot look at,
a malignant purpose in a nun's eye.

Who was the last man on earth,
to whom the cold cloud brought the blood to his face?
Numbly I climb to the mountain-tops of ours
where my own soul quivers on the edge of answers.

Which still, stale air sits on an angel's wings?
What holds my rain so it's hard to overcome?

I Hear My Fingers Sadly Touching
an Ivory Key

Swans sink wordlessly to the carpet
miles of polished floors
reach out
for the glass of voices

There are gulls crying everywhere
and glazed green grass
in the park with the swans
folding their cold throats

23

Hunger

It was hard to believe the flesh was heavy on my back.
The fisherman said: will you have her, carelessly,
trailing his nets and his nerves, as though his words
sanctified the purpose with which he faced himself.
I saw his white bone thrash his eyes.

I followed him across the sprawling sands,
my mind thumping in the flesh's sling.
Hope lay perhaps in burning the house I lived in.
Silence gripped my sleeves; his body clawed
at the froth his old nets had dragged up from the seas.

In the flickering dark his lean-to opened like a wound.
The wind was I, and the days and nights before.
Palm fronds scratched my skin. Inside the shack
an oil lamp splayed the hours bunched to those walls.
Over and over the sticky soot crossed the space of my mind.

I heard him say: my daughter, she's just turned fifteen. . . .
Feel her. I'll be back soon, your bus leaves at nine.
The sky fell on me, and a father's exhausted wile.
Long and lean, her years were cold as rubber.
She opened her wormy legs wide. I felt the hunger there,
the other one, the fish slithering, turning inside.

Hands

Between them
a silence occupies the whole place.

Slowly my body has walked
into deep water.

As a boy I learned to come in
by the back door. Sad
houses now, clean and leaning
against one another, full of sleep.

My old rag elephant is
smothered with small screams.

From the dark surface,
waving like grass—
When the last boat crosses the lake.

The Moon Moments

The faint starlight rolls restlessly on the mat.
Those women talking outside have clouds passing across their eyes.
Always there is a moon that is taking me somewhere.
Why does one room invariably lead into other rooms?

We, opening in time our vague doors,
convinced that our minds lead to something never allowed before,
sit down hurt under the trees, feeding it simply because
it is there, as the wind does, blowing against the tree.

Yet time is not clairvoyant,
and if it has the answer to our lives, proud
in its possession of that potential which can change our natures,
beating the visions of childhood out of us,

the socialism and the love,
until we remain awkwardly swung to the great north of honour.
What humility is that which will not let me reveal the real?
What shameful secret lies hidden in the shadows of my moon?

All these years; our demands no longer hurt our eyes.
How can I stop the life I lead within myself—
The startled, pleading question in my hands lying in my lap
while the gods go by, triumphant, in the sacked city at midnight?

25

JAYANTA MAHAPATRA

A Kind of Happiness

The boat I've laid my mind on
is adrift, moving slowly up an ageless creek,
through water still and colourless as time,
among drifts of uncomprehending silent reeds.

In it I've staked those my precious years,
the fear of the depths and the unholy cold;
now for that reason maybe (being so awake)
I fear it may never reach the promise of the sea.

There is a hand I remember, that lay simply
in your lap, warm and sacred and drenched
with its promise, a hair's breadth away from my own,
yet some spell did not drop anchor, to lay mine on it,

barely escaping happiness I thought I knew of it,
but would I recognize it if it really came?
What use would it be if I'd tie the boat to a tree
and lie down in the heart of its demand?

It soaks into each song, words and the throats of birds
hoping such symbols would make up its definition,
yet can the good world
hold the flowing movement of fear in the mind?

Can slain men show the miracle of being alive?
Always it's this boat that nails me to the water,
darkening its silent waste and flow,
the reeds merciless like those dead,
yet don't I know it is better to leave the boat alone?

What would tell me at last where I belong?
The cracking keel, the bold green moss?

The Door

This thing
wakes me like a hand.

Grass waits

and rock
takes the wind's place.

Huge door
drifting
with feet of light,

my eyes
quietly open
before the night's.

The Abandoned British Cemetery at Balasore

This is history.
I would not disturb it: the ruins of stone and marble,
the crumbling wall of brick, the coma of alienated decay.
How exactly should the archaic dead make me behave?

A hundred and fifty years ago
I might have lived. Now nothing offends my ways.
A quietness of bramble and grass holds me to a weed.
Will it matter if I know who the victims were, who survived?

And yet, awed by the forgotten dead,
I walk around them: thirty-nine graves, their legends
floating in a twilight of baleful littoral,
the flaking history my intrusion does not animate.

Awkward in the silence, a scrawny lizard
watches the drama with its shrewd, hooded gaze.
And a scorpion, its sting drooping,
two eerie arms spread upon the marble, over an alien name.

In the circle the epitaphs run: Florence R——, darling wife
of Captain R—— R——, aged nineteen, of cholera . . .
Helen, beloved daughter of Mr. & Mrs. ——, of cholera,
aged seventeen, in the year of our Lord, eighteen hundred . . .

Of what concern to me is a vanished Empire?
Or the conquest of my ancestors' timeless ennui?
It is the dying young who have the power to show
what the heart will hide, the grass shows no more.

Who watches now in the dark near the dead wall?
The tribe of grass in the cracks of my eyes?
It is the cholera still, death's sickly trickle,
that plagues the sleepy shacks beyond this hump of earth,

moving easily, swiftly, with quick power
through both past and present, the increasing young,
into the final bone, wearying all truth with ruin.
This is the iron

rusting in the vanquished country, the blood's unease,
the useless rain upon my familiar window;
the tired triumphant smile left behind by the dead
on a discarded anchor half-sunk in mud beside the graves:

out there on the earth's unwavering gravity
where it waits like a deity perhaps
for the elaborate ceremonial of a coming generation
to keep history awake, stifle the survivor's issuing cry.

The Captive Air of Chandipur-on-Sea

Day after day the drunk sea at Chandipur
spits out the gauze wings of shells along the beach
and rumples the thin air behind the sands.
Who can tell of the songs of this sea that go on
to baffle and double the space around our lives?
Or of smells paralysed through the centuries,
of deltas hard and white that stretched once
to lure the feet of women bidding their men goodbye?
Or of salt and light that dark and provocative eyes
demanded, their shoulders drooping like lotuses
in the noonday sun?

And what is it now that scatters the tide
in the shadow of this proud watercourse?
The ridicule of the dead?
Susurrant sails still whisper
legends on the horizon: who are you,
occupant of the silent sigh of the conch?
The ground seems only a memory now, a torn breath,
and as we wait for the tide to flood the mudflats
the song that reaches our ears is just our own.
The cries of fishermen come drifting through the spray,
music of what the world has lost.

Of that Love

Of that love, of that mile
walked together in the rain,
only a weariness remains.

I am that stranger now
my mirror holds to me;
the moment's silence
hardly moves across the glass
I pity myself in another's guise.

And no one's back here, no one
I can recognize, and from my side
I see nothing. Years have passed
since I sat with you, watching
the sky grow lonelier with cloudlessness,
waiting for your body to make it lived in.

The Vase

The strong south wind hits our faces again,
it's October;
sunsets are fiery red
and the waters of wells are clear already—
there we are, under the mango tree,
in the old house, amid the drift of things,
the vase on the bookcase
with shadows of swifts reeling round it,
and we don't know whether we are alone any more.

But each day
we watch the swifts come and go,
watch the still-slender, teasing whore
who shuffles down the crowded road and finds out
that the middle-aged man surreptitiously following her
is only listening to the slowing sounds
of his own heart; and we sit and long
for the child who left in 'seventy-three,
and behave like our bitch that catches a scent
and sniffs about in the air.

We look around today and the day after tomorrow,
remembering those who caught us like irrigation-canals
across the dry nights in the distant countryside,
and remembering, suddenly, someone
who once envied us and our bodies,
so impudent, glistening with rain.

Ah, this voice I hear now,
what answer do I owe you?
The tree trembles in the wind,
the house where we once made love
now weakens at the knees. And all the time
that gathered into those moments
fills the grave of the vast vase with dust.

Days

These days.
They are long and don't end.
I pretend.
If the days had only robbed me
I would have been in a rage.
But where's my anger now?
The days merely contain.
Come, wave to me, I coax my day,
the way one waves to a little child.
But it doesn't seem to go away.
The days are not even in the way.

Leaning against a tree
I am one with the sky.
There may have been days
I followed for a while
as they softened in the light,
those I found among the shadows of my life.
A day behind the door,
one keeping watch;
another a ghost
wandering in the garden.
And one probably anxious to return.

These days.
Sometimes they just move my mind
a little.
Like cattle crossing a road,
they pause without knowing
and stare beyond them,
then walk on.

Waiting

I sit here, waiting for her, sit here
with the empty skin drooping over my shoulders
as I had sat waiting many times before
beside the same window, in the same old chair.
Once in a while I'd open my notebooks,
find the words I had written float away
into the wilderness on the other side of the paper.
Like the smoke drifting over the burning-ground
of my own flesh. I shut my tired eyes.
And I try not to think of the quick warm skin
of the eighteen-year-old girl I met last month.
I stretch my lonely lips into an unforgivable grin.
I turn my face over in the darkness of my room
and peer into it; but I don't remember now
when my beard started to grow,
I let the minute drop the hour to the ground;
but each time it came back, and I had to do this
all over again, to put my mind at ease.
I touch my shoulders; they are bare, contrite.
Like the shape of a deserted park bench in the rain.
Was some sort of change coming over me?
Or was it time's empty skin, waiting for an excuse
to advance the blood, to keep it occupied?
My notebooks are there, my pretty wife too,
but I have been with them long, long in love,
and they have worn me slowly around the edges.
Or maybe it isn't because of *them*, themselves;

it is because of where I came from, and of
what I suddenly realized I was really waiting for:
the life that my life seeks, when I go in
to answer it; but it had gone the other way
to where I couldn't meet it at all,
as I go back to where I was, by the same window,
without a word, waiting for her,
empty skin flapping like truce flags in a losing war.

A. K. Ramanujan

Attippat Krishnaswami Ramanujan was born in Mysore in 1929 and educated at Maharaja's College, Mysore, Deccan College, Poona, and Indiana University. He has taught at the University of Chicago since 1962, and is currently professor in the Department of South Asian Languages and Civilizations, the Department of Linguistics, and the Committee on Social Thought. Ramanujan is the author of more than fifteen books, which include verse in English and Kannada: *The Striders* (1966), *Relations* (1971), *Selected Poems* (1976), *Second Sight* (1986), *Hokkulalli Huvilla* (No Lotus in the Navel, 1969), *Mattu Itara Padyagalu* (And Other Poems, 1977); translations of verse and prose from Tamil and Kannada: *The Interior Landscape* (1967), *Speaking of Siva* (1972), *Samskara* (1976), *Hymns for the Drowning* (1981), *Poems of Love and War* (1985); and a co-edited volume each on folklore and Indian literatures. Ramanujan was awarded the Padma Shri in 1976, a MacArthur Prize Fellowship in 1983, and was recently elected a Fellow of the American Academy of Arts and Sciences.

Like tricky Chinese boxes, A. K. Ramanujan's poems are difficult to open but of exquisite workmanship; they're objects to hold between fingers as much as they are printed lines to read with the eyes. You sense this from even the way they appear on the page, the left-hand margin carefully jagged, and the overall design often original to the poem. In this he resembles that other inventor of stanzas, George Herbert, who, it is worth remembering especially here, wrote 'My thoughts are all a case of knives'.

'It is interesting to speculate', W. H. Auden says in a footnote to his essay on Tennyson, 'on the relation between the strictness and musicality of a poet's form and his own anxiety. It may well be, I think, that the more he is conscious of an inner disorder and dread, the more value he will place on tidiness in the work as a *defense*...' Each time we read Ramanujan—whose work has the tidiness of a prize-winning garden and who concludes 'Anxiety' by saying 'anxiety / can find no metaphor to end it'—we speculate on that relation afresh. Something must give way if the poem is to come through; equally, someone has to make the imaginative leap into it.

34

Ramanujan's defence, like Wallace Stevens's, is severe, but there are openings too for those who want to look for them. Unable to get in some days, I visualize conversation with him. Quoting Robert Lowell's line in 'Epilogue', ' "Yet why not say what happened?" ' I ask. And he replies, 'But I have.'

Ramanujan's theme is the inadequacy of masks and the necessity of having them, and in this instance the mask is identical with the face. If anything, his damascened strophes are given a keener edge by the kniving thoughts behind them, for these are poems instinct with violence. Being more astute than other poets, Ramanujan's mask is overpowering and, at the same time, almost not there, as in this section from 'Entries from a Catalogue of Fears':

> Add now, at thirty-nine, to the old old fear
>   of depths and heights,
>   of father in the bedroom,
>   insects, iodine
>   in the eye,
>   sudden knives and urchin laughter
>   in the redlight alley,
>   add now
>   the men in line
>   behind my daughter.

The tone, that of someone calling out numbers from a ledger; the catalogue within a catalogue; and the pattern, invented for the occasion, of the stanza itself, effectively shut us out of the poem. Having done so, the speaker, almost as an afterthought, adds a last fear: 'add now / the men in line / behind my daughter'. After a succession of masks, we are now looking straight into his anxious iodine-free eyes. We could have missed them altogether; indeed, he may half wish we had.

To say, as one critic does, that the poems 'are based on the cultural predicament of a person who has been brought up in a traditional culture, and is now living in a very different' one, is to misjudge the action.[1] For as Ramanujan shuttles between 'Smalltown, South India' and 'The traffic light . . . / on 57th and Dorchester', between a river in Madurai and Lake Michigan, between slipper and alewife,

[1] S. Nagarajan in *Contemporary Poets*, 4th edition, ed. James Vinson and D. L. Kirkpatrick, London, 1985, 689.

35

nothing really changes for him except the back-cloth in the long-running play of himself. This element of drama (watched by his Upanishadic 'watchers . . . from their nowhere perches' in *Second Sight*), together with some of his bizarre costumes ('I rise among them, / mud on my nose, / a rhododendron rising from a compost / of rhododendrons'), save him from solipsism. Ramanujan's critics pay scant attention also to the small cunning ways, like sometimes spelling *Hindu* with two o's, by which he distances himself from the very culture he was born into. Behind his self-absorbed look and regulated life, the Hindoo in 'The Hindoo: the Only Risk' is a dangerous humbug. Ramanujan puts it more mildly, which makes it worse:

> At the bottom of all this bottomless
> enterprise to keep simple the heart's given beat,
>
> the only risk is heartlessness.

In 'Some Indian Uses of History on a Rainy Day', a 'Professor of Sanskrit / on cultural exchange' wanders about a European city in the rain, unable to read the simplest signs 'on door, bus, and shop'. Suddenly he recognizes one on somebody's arm, and feels he is not among strangers after all. The sign is the swastika; the city, Berlin; the year, 1935. The risks in being 'Hindoo' can only increase. 'I must seek and will find / my particular hell only in my hindu mind', Ramanujan writes in 'Conventions of Despair'. Even here, in a passage his parochial followers are quick to refer to, the burden is the racked mind; 'hindu', with a small h, a big red herring.

Ramanujan's third collection, *Second Sight*, is more like a free-ranging commentary on a private book. The poems, for this reason, may lack the immediacy of lyrics, and we cannot always put our finger on the emotion that triggered them off. As in the example from 'Entries from a Catalogue of Fears', unhurried tone and deliberate manner are everything here, almost everything:

> Composed as I am, like others,
> of elements on certain well-known lists,
> father's seed and mother's egg
>
> gathering earth, air, fire, mostly
> water, into a mulberry mass,
> moulding calcium,

carbon, even gold, magnesium and such,
  into a chattering self tangled
in love and work . . .

                         ('Elements of Composition')

There are, among the elements, fugitive moments that mirror the self's own divided condition:

        . . . a legend half-heard
      in a train

      of a half-man searching
        for an ever-fleeing
      other half

Finally, near the poem's end, the voice of the concealed, evasive figure breaks through the artifice: 'and even as I add, / I lose, decompose'. This cry is heard, with slight changes ('Losing everytime I win'), in several other poems written in the same three-line stanza; its paradox binds *Second Sight*.

In 'Highway Stripper', the 'chattering self' disappears from our field of vision altogether. We feel quite naked without clothes, but without disguises even more so. The former condition doesn't rob us of our identity as completely as the latter does. In the event, the stripper throws away both, which still leaves him at the wheel of his 'once-blue Mustang', 'rushing forever / towards a perfect / coupling / with naked nothing'.

Disappearance, however, is a form of expression. At one point in the book, the author, trickster, juryman, makes off with the lines themselves and still leaves a complete poem behind (see 'On the Death of a Poem' below). If it is true that to add is to lose and decompose, then its opposite is not less true: that to decompose is to return, once again, to the elements of composition. Which is why the naked stripper, though he may never get there, rushes to couple with 'naked nothing'; which is also why Ramanujan, while sentencing a poem, gives it life.

A. K. RAMANUJAN

The Striders

And search
for certain thin-
stemmed, bubble-eyed water bugs.
See them perch
on dry capillary legs
weightless
on the ripple skin
of a stream.

No, not only prophets
walk on water. This bug sits
on a landslide of lights
and drowns eye-
deep
into its tiny strip
of sky.

'Strider' is the New England name for the water insect in this poem.

Breaded Fish

Specially for me, she had some breaded
fish; even thrust a blunt-headed
smelt into my mouth;

and looked hurt when I could
neither sit nor eat, as a hood
of memory like a coil on a heath

opened in my eyes: a dark half-naked
length of woman, dead
on the beach in a yard of cloth,

dry, rolled by the ebb, breaded
by the grained indifference of sand. I headed
for the shore, my heart beating in my mouth.

Looking for a Cousin on a Swing

When she was four or five
she sat on a village swing
and her cousin, six or seven,
sat himself against her;
with every lunge of the swing
she felt him
in the lunging pits
of her feeling;
              and afterwards
we climbed a tree, she said,

not very tall, but full of leaves
like those of a figtree,

and we were very innocent
about it.

Now she looks for the swing
in cities with fifteen suburbs
and tries to be innocent
about it

not only on the crotch of a tree
that looked as if it would burst
under every leaf
into a brood of scarlet figs

if someone suddenly sneezed.

Self-Portrait

I resemble everyone
but myself, and sometimes see
in shop-windows,
    despite the well-known laws
    of optics,
the portrait of a stranger,
date unknown,
often signed in a corner
by my father.

Anxiety

Not branchless as the fear tree,
it has naked roots and secret twigs.
Not geometric as the parabolas
of hope, it has loose ends
with a knot at the top
that's me.
                Not wakeful in its white-snake
glassy ways like the eloping gaiety of waters,
it drowses, viscous and fibered as pitch.

Flames have only lungs. Water is all eyes.
The earth has bone for muscle. And the air
is a flock of invisible pigeons.
                            But anxiety
can find no metaphor to end it.

Case History

What had he done
to crush glass in his fist
one middle-aged morning, known

only as morning by clocks without the sun?
At seven, his slingshot had not hit
the frosted childhood's streetlight:

he was no looting horseback Hun
out of his history books. On
evenings full of bats' wings

he had scarcely seen a sister raped by a dead father's sin
but only shaped by a mother's word. In
the swirl of his teens he had perhaps thrilled

to raisin-thefts and one kiss under the stairs. Once he ran
from a body-house without windows
looking for the wombs of faceless women

he never filled
with sons. But now he has glass in his fist
and several rows

of futures that could not reach any past.

Love Poem for a Wife. 2

After a night of rage
that lasted days,
quarrels in a forest,
waterfalls, exchanges, marriage,
exploration of bays
and places
we had never known
we would ever know,

my wife's always
changing syriac face,
chosen of all faces,
a pouting difficult child's

changing in the chameleon
emerald
wilderness of Kerala,
small cousin to tall

mythic men, rubberplant
and peppervine,
frocks with print patterns
copied locally
from the dotted
butterfly,
grandmother wearing white
day and night in a village

full of the colour schemes
of kraits and gartersnakes;
adolescent in Aden among stabbing
Arabs, betrayed and whipped
yet happy among ships
in harbour,
and the evacuees,
the borrowed earth

under the borrowed trees;
taught dry and wet,
hot and cold
by the monsoons then,
by the siroccos now
on copper
dustcones, the crater
townships in the volcanoes

of Aden:
        I dreamed one day
that face my own yet hers,
with my own nowhere
to be found; lost; cut
loose like my dragnet
past.

I woke up and groped,
turned on the realism

of the ceiling light,
found half a mirror
in the mountain cabin
fallen behind the dresser
to look at my face now
and the face
of her sleep, still asleep
and very syriac on the bed

behind: happy for once
at such loss of face,
whole in the ambivalence
of being halfwoman half-
man contained in a common
body,
androgynous as a god
balancing stillness in the middle

of a duel to make it dance:
soon to be myself, a man
unhappy in the morning
to be himself again,
the past still there,
a drying
net on the mountain,

in the morning, in the waking
my wife's face still fast
asleep, blessed as by
butterfly, snake, shiprope,
and grandmother's other
children,
by my only love's only
insatiable envy.

The Hindoo: the Only Risk

Just to keep the heart's simple given beat
through a neighbour's striptease or a friend's suicide.
To keep one's hand away from the kitchen knife

through that returning weekly need
to maim oneself or carve up wife
and child. Always and everywhere, to eat

three square meals at regular hours; suppress
that itch to take a peek at the dead street-
dog before the scavengers come. Not to be caught

dead at sea, battle, riot, adultery or hate
nor between the rollers of a giant lathe. Yes,
to keep it cool when strangers' children hiss

as if they knew what none could know nor guess.
At the bottom of all this bottomless
enterprise to keep simple the heart's given beat,

the only risk is heartlessness.

Snakes and Ladders

Losing everytime I win, climbing
    ladders, falling to the bottom with snakes,
I make scenes:

in my anger, I smash all transparent
    things, crystal, glass panes, one-way mirrors,
and my glasses,

blinding myself, I hit my head on white
    walls, shut myself up in the bathroom,
toying with razors,

44

till I see blood on my thumb, when I
    black out, a child again in a glass booth
elevator, plummeting

to the earth five floors a second,
    taking my sky, turning cloud, and San Francisco
down to the ground,

where, sick to my stomach, I wake
    wide open, hugging the white toilet bowl,
my cool porcelain sister.

On the Death of a Poem

Images consult
one
another,

a conscience-
stricken
jury,

and come
slowly
to a sentence.

Highway Stripper

Once as I was travelling
on a highway
to Mexico
behind a battered once-blue
Mustang
with a dusty rear window,
the wind really sang
for me

when suddenly
out of the side
of the speeding car
in front of me
a woman's hand
with a wrist-watch on it
threw away
a series of whirling objects
on to the hurtling road:

a straw
hat,
a white shoe fit
to be a fetish,
then another,
a heavy pleated skirt
and a fluttery
slip, faded pink,
frayed lace-edge
and all
(I even heard it swish),
a leg-of-mutton blouse
just as fluttery.

And as I stepped
on the gas
and my car lunged
into the fifty feet
between me
and them,
a rather ordinary,
used, and off-white bra
for smallish
breasts whirled off
the window
and struck
a farmer's barbed wire
with yellow-green wheat grass
beyond

and spread-eagled on it,
pinned
by the blowing wind.

Then before I knew,
bright red panties
laced with white
hit
my windshield
and I flinched,
I swerved,
but then
it was gone,
swept aside
before I straightened up—
fortunately, no one else
on the road:

excited, curious
to see the stripper
on the highway,
maybe with an urgent
lover's one free hand
(or were there more?)
on her breast
or thigh,
I stepped again
on the gas, frustrated by their
dusty rear window
at fifty feet,
I passed them
at seventy.

In that absolute
second,
that glimpse and after-
image in this hell
of voyeurs, I saw

47

only one at the wheel:
a man,
about forty,

a spectacled profile
looking only
at the road
beyond the nose
of his Mustang,
with a football
radio on.

again and again
I looked
in my rearview
mirror
as I steadied my pace

against the circling trees,
but there was only
a man:

had he stripped
not only hat
and blouse, shoes
and panties
and bra,
had he shed maybe
even the woman
he was wearing,

or was it me
moulting, shedding
vestiges,
old investments,
rushing forever
towards a perfect

A. K. RAMANUJAN

coupling
with naked nothing
in a world
without places?

Moulting

Moulting has first to find a thorn at a suitable height to
pin and fix the growing numbness in the tail. Then it can begin
to slough and move out of that loose end, whole though flayed
alive.

That's how you see now and then a dry skin or two hanging,
and you may be sickened for a minute by a thin old snake
vacillating and pale on a black thorn, working out a new body on
a fence you just defiled.

Lord of snakes and eagles, and everything in between, cover
my son with an hour's shade and be the thorn at a suitable height
in his hour of change.

Chicago Zen

i

Now tidy your house,
dust especially your living room

and do not forget to name
all your children.

ii

Watch your step. Sight may strike you
blind in unexpected places.

The traffic light turns orange
on 57th and Dorchester, and you stumble,

49

you fall into a vision of forest fires,
enter a frothing Himalayan river,

rapid, silent.

On the 14th floor,
Lake Michigan crawls and crawls

in the window. Your thumbnail
cracks a lobster louse on the windowpane

from your daughter's hair
and you drown, eyes open,

towards the Indies, the antipodes.
And you, always so perfectly sane.

iii

Now you know what you always knew:
the country cannot be reached

by jet. Nor by boat on jungle river,
hashish behind the Monkey-temple,

nor moonshot to the cratered Sea
of Tranquillity, slim circus girls

on a tightrope between tree and tree
with white parasols, or the one

and only blue guitar.

Nor by any
other means of transport,

migrating with a clean valid passport,
no, not even by transmigrating

without any passport at all,
but only by answering ordinary

black telephones, questions
walls and small children ask,

and answering all calls of nature.

iv

Watch your step, watch it, I say,
especially at the first high
threshold,

                    and the sudden low
one near the end
of the flight
of stairs,

          and watch
for the last
step that's never there.

Arun Kolatkar

Arun Balkrishna Kolatkar was born in Kolhapur in 1932 and educated at Rajaram High School Branch, Kolhapur. In an unpublished autobiographical essay written in 1987, he describes the house in which he spent his first seventeen years:

> I grew up in a house with nine rooms that were arranged, well almost, like a house of cards. Five in a row on the ground, topped by three on the first, and one on the second floor.
>
> The place wasn't quite as cheerful as playing cards, though. Or as colourful. All the rooms had mudfloors which had to be plastered with cowdung every week to keep them in good repair. All the walls were painted . . . in some indeterminate colour which I can only describe as a lighter shade of sulphurous yellow.

It was in one of these rooms—his father's study on the first floor—that Kolatkar found 'a hidden treasure'. It consisted of

> three or four packets of glossy black and white picture postcards showing the monuments and architectural marvels of Greece, as well as sculptures from the various museums of Italy and France.
>
> As I sat in my father's chair, examining the contents of his drawers, it was inevitable that I should've been introduced to the finest achievements of Baroque and Renaissance art, the works of people like Bernini and Michelangelo, and I spent long hours spellbound by their art.
>
> But at the same time I must make a confession. The European girls disappointed me. They have beautiful faces, great figures, and they showed it all. But there was nothing to see. I looked blankly at their smooth, creaseless, and apparently scratch-resistant crotches, sighed, and moved on to the next picture.
>
> The boys, too. They let it all hang out, but were hardly what you might call well-hung. David, for example. Was it David? Great muscles, great body, but his penis was like a tiny little mouse. Move on. Next picture.

Kolatkar enrolled at the J. J. School of Art, Bombay, in 1949. Afterwards, he also attended art schools in Kolhapur and Pune, finally taking a Diploma in Painting from the J. J. School in 1957.

He writes in both English and Marathi, and although his poems have appeared in magazines and anthologies since 1955, he has so far published only two books, *Jejuri* (1976), in English, and *Arun Kolatkarchya Kavita* (1976), in Marathi. 'the boatride', a long poem in eleven sections first published in *damn you* / 6 in 1968, is available in the anthologies edited by Saleem Peeradina and R. Parthasarathy (see select bibliography). A German translation, by Giovanni Bandini, of *Jejuri* was published by Verlag Wolf Mersch in 1984. Kolatkar works in advertising and lives in Bombay.

Few would know that some of Kolatkar's early poems in English appeared in *An Anthology of Marathi Poetry: 1945–1965* (1967), edited by Dilip Chitre. (Chitre makes some very perceptive comments on them in the introduction to the book.) Though both 'Woman' and 'Suicide of Rama' say 'English version by the poet', their Marathi originals were never committed to paper.[1] This bit of deception, by itself a minor bibliographical fact, raises a host of complex issues centred round the idea of the poet, especially in our century, as a wanderer across language.[2] Kolatkar himself operates across the two he writes in, sending out, as we have just seen, occasional false signals. On the other hand, certain of his poems are dually located. The Marathi texts of 'Irani Restaurant Bombay', 'Crabs', and 'Biograph' are to be found in *Arun Kolatkarchya Kavita*, while, simultaneously, they are poems in English, smuggled into the language through the unmanned checkpoint of verse. A second reason of these poems' neglect is, of course, *Jejuri*, the book Kolatkar has come to be identified with.

Not only is *Jejuri* among the finest single poems written in India in the past forty years, few books of verse published here have been so successful. It won the Commonwealth Poetry Prize, and quickly went into three editions. But the editions were small and the distribution limited. This is unfortunate, as no selection of the thirty-one poems in the sequence can hope to convey the leisurely pace of the whole; how, while seeming to be straight as a road, it makes an enchanted circle, one the reader cannot escape from even if he wants to (see 'The Railway Station' below).

Since *Jejuri* takes all its images from a temple town of the same name near Pune in western Maharashtra, and has a picture of

---

[1] *An Anthology of Marathi Poetry: 1945–1965*, Bombay, 1967, 136–7.

[2] See George Steiner, *Extraterritorial: Papers on Literature and the Language Revolution*, London, Faber and Faber, 1972.

Khandoba—a form of Shiva worshipped by Maharashtra's Dhangar community—on the cover, simple academic critics have confused the poem with the place, and followed it as a work that indicates the poet's attitude towards religion—in the narrow sense of the word. Asked by an interviewer whether he believed in God, Kolatkar replied, 'I leave the question alone. I don't think I have to take a position about God one way or the other.'[3]

The presiding deity of *Jejuri* is not Khandoba, but the human eye. Kolatkar, who has also designed the book, places the illustration emblematic of the text at the back. It is based on the last poem of the sequence (see section 6 of 'The Railway Station' below), and shows the ball of the sun suspended above a railway track that meets at infinity. The theme of a poem resides in its lines rather than within state boundaries, and *Jejuri's* lines are acts of looking (the sun) at the physical world (the railway track). They name and observe, isolate and magnify, and by so doing radically transform—or in Rilke's phrase, 'make glorious'—everything they see.

'Things', Proust said, 'are gods.' And Kolatkar,

> No more a place of worship this place
> is nothing less than the house of god.
>
> ('Heart of Ruin')

In a writer, reverence towards things already makes for a certain objectivity and exactness. He may approach these divinities, but not throw himself on them, nor confuse one with another, for no two are alike. The passionate masters of this new faith—Kolatkar's precursors—were Ezra Pound, William Carlos Williams, Louis Zukofsky, to mention only poets, and only Americans.

Details are the cornerstones of our visual world. Remove them, and it sinks to the ground, is a blur. For training the eyes, *Jejuri* is as fine a school as any:

> That's no doorstep.
> It's a pillar on its side.
>
> Yes.
> That's what it is.
>
> ('The Doorstep')

[3] Quoted in Bruce King, *Modern Indian Poetry in English*, Delhi, 1987, 170.

This is the whole poem. It surprises by revealing the familiar, the hidden that is always before us. Other poems tell of forms and patterns that vanish even as they appear:

> It's a little yellow butterfly.
> It has taken these wretched hills
> under its wings.
>
> Just a pinch of yellow,
> it opens before it closes
> and closes before it o
>
> where is it
>
> ('The Butterfly')

You do, however, go through life without noticing little yellow butterflies, far less stone pillars lying on their side, till one day some trucker coming down the road at full tilt brings you to your senses, 'Can't you see where you going you motherfucker?' (see 'Biograph' below; interestingly, the line in the Marathi text is in Hindi, दिखता नही मादरचोद दिखता नही). The trucker may not have read *Jejuri*, but at least knows what is in front of him. Or he'd be a dead man the next minute. More likely, it would be you.

Woman

a woman may collect cats read thrillers
her insomnia may seep through the great walls of history
a lizard may paralyse her
a sewing machine may bend her
moonlight may intercept the bangle
circling her wrist

a woman may name her cats
the circulating library
may lend her new thrillers

a spiked man may impale her
a woman may add
a new recipe to her scrapbook

judiciously distilling her whimper the city lights
may declare it null and void
in a prodigious weather
above a darkling woman
surgeons may shoot up and explode
in a weather fraught with forceps
a woman may damn
man

a woman may shave her legs regularly
a woman may take up landscape painting
a woman may poison
twenty three cockroaches

Suicide of Rama

winding verses stir him up
the turreted epic shrugs him off
the river resumes him
from legend's ledge the hero falls

the crescent cuts a rope of fables
we cloud the skeleton with folklore
from valmiki's roof top rama jumps
disturbing a tile or two

his flesh of myth saponified
his arse turned up toward the moon
rama drifts like a gourd
far from sap or shore

man leaves his legend standing
one wave bears the other out
the river refers his bones
to the salt judgement of the sea

Irani Restaurant Bombay

the cockeyed shah of iran watches the cake
decompose carefully in the cracked showcase;
distracted only by a fly on the make
as it finds in a loafer's wrist an operational base.

dogmatically green and elaborate trees defeat
breeze. the crooked swan begs pardon
if it disturb the pond; the road neat
as a needle points at a lovely cottage with a garden.

the thirsty loafer sees the stylised perfection
of such a landscape in a glass of water wobble
a sticky tea print for his scholarly attention
singles out a verse from the blank testament of the table.

an instant of mirrors turns the tables on space.
while promoting darkness under the chair, the cat
in its two timing sleep dreams evenly and knows
dreaming as an administrative problem. his cigarette

57

lit, the loafer, affecting the exactitude of a pedagogue
places the match in the tea circles and sees it rise:
as when to identify a corpse one visits a morgue
and politely the corpse rises from a block of ice.

the burnt match with the tea circle makes a rude
compass. the heretic needle jabs a black star.
tables, chairs, mirrors are night that needs to be sewed
and cashier is where at seams it comes apart.

Crabs

Look, look.
Just look at them.
The crabs.
There are two of them.

They're keeping watch.
On whom, you ask?
On you of course,
who else?

See how they're looking?
Looking at you,
naturally.
And you'll never catch them blink either.

One on this side.
One on the other.
At an angle of a hundred and sixty degrees
to your left and to your right.

They're going to eat your eyes.
That scare you?
It needn't, you know.
It's not as if they're going to start eating right away.

No. But one of these days.
Tomorrow? Who knows?
If not tomorrow, then the day after.
Or ten years from now, who can tell?

They're in no hurry.
They have plenty of time.
And they can live without food
for a long time, you know.

Look this way,
quick.
Don't turn your head.
Just move your eyeballs.

Do you see a crab there?
Not the whole crab, may be,
not yet,
but you did see something move?

Now look the other way.
No, no. Not the whole head.
Just move your eyeballs
like I said.

All you can see for now
is just the pincers may be,
but you'll see,
you'll see the whole crab yet.

And you'll see it clearly.
They're only doing their job of course,
but patience
is one thing you should learn from them.

The crabs belong to you,
and to you alone.
They have no interest in eating
somebody else's eyes.

59

They came out of your head.
Where else did you think they came from?
But how they've grown.
Look at them now,

big fat crabs.
They've been playing a waiting game
ever since they emerged
from your head.

They'll come for your eyes
any time you say.
Sometimes I think they're just waiting
for your permission.

All you have to do is give the word.
And once they've eaten your eyes,
their job is done.
You'll never see them again.

Biograph

Knotting the cord, the midwife said,
It's a boy, it's a boy, it's a boy.
Piercing an earlobe, the goldsmith said,
Two bucks, just two bucks.
Syringe in hand, the nurse said,
It's not gonna hurt, not a bit.

Measuring my dick, Baban said,
Mine's bigger, bigger than yours.
Punching my back, Baban said,
My dad can lick your dad.
Kicking my shin, Baban said,
Sissy, a sissy, what a sissy you are.

60

ARUN KOLATKAR

Pressing her toes against mine, Bunny said,
Bicycle, bicycle, let's play bicycle.
Rubbing spittle on my tummy, Bunny said,
Doctor, doctor, let's play doctor.
Tickling my ribs, Bunny said,
Come on in, between the sheets.

Boxing my ears, a teacher said,
How much is thirty three times thirty eight?
Rapping my knuckles, a teacher said,
And where's Sheffield then? Where's Sheffield?
Squeezing my thigh, a teacher said,
Let's go to the mango grove.

Twisting my neck, the barber said,
Don't move now, don't move.
Measuring my chest, the tailor said,
Thirty one inches, just thirty one.
Forcing my foot into the shoe, the cobbler said,
Use it, and it won't be so tight.

Jumping on my back, junior said,
Giddyup, giddyup.
Giving me the boot, my boss said,
I can't help it Mr. Nene, I just can't.
Grabbing my cock, my wife said,
I'll chop it off one day, just chop it off.

Feeling my balls, a doctor said,
Hydrocele, I'm sure it's hydrocele.
Sticking a pin in my toe, another said,
Leprosy, you can take it from me, it's leprosy.
Tapping my stomach, a third one said,
Ulcer, ulcer, no doubt about it.

Stepping on my toes, a guy said,
Sorry man, I'm sorry.
Sticking an umbrella in my eye, another said,
I hope you aren't hurt.
Bearing down on me, full tilt, a trucker said,
Can't you see where you going you motherfucker?

61

from *Jejuri*

The Bus

The tarpaulin flaps are buttoned down
on the windows of the state transport bus
all the way up to Jejuri.

A cold wind keeps whipping
and slapping a corner of the tarpaulin
at your elbow.

You look down the roaring road.
You search for signs of daybreak in
what little light spills out of the bus.

Your own divided face in a pair of glasses
on an old man's nose
is all the countryside you get to see.

You seem to move continually forward
towards a destination
just beyond the caste mark between his eyebrows.

Outside, the sun has risen quietly.
It aims through an eyelet in the tarpaulin
and shoots at the old man's glasses.

A sawed off sunbeam comes to rest
gently against the driver's right temple.
The bus seems to change direction.

At the end of the bumpy ride
with your own face on either side
when you get off the bus

you don't step inside the old man's head.

Heart of Ruin

The roof comes down on Maruti's head.
Nobody seems to mind.

Least of all Maruti himself.
May be he likes a temple better this way.

A mongrel bitch has found a place
for herself and her puppies

in the heart of the ruin.
May be she likes a temple better this way.

The bitch looks out at you guardedly
past a doorway cluttered with broken tiles.

The pariah puppies tumble over her.
May be they like a temple better this way.

The black eared puppy has gone a little too far.
A tile clicks under its foot.

It's enough to strike terror in the heart
of a dung beetle

and send him running for cover
to the safety of the broken collection box

that never did get a chance to get out
from under the crushing weight of the roof beam.

No more a place of worship this place
is nothing less than the house of god.

6

ARUN KOLATKAR

Chaitanya[1]

come off it
said chaitanya to a stone
in stone language

wipe the red paint off your face
i don't think the colour suits you
i mean what's wrong
with being just a plain stone
i'll still bring you flowers
you like the flowers of zendu
don't you
i like them too

[1] Vaishnavite Bengali saint and reformer, said to have visited Jejuri in 1510–11.

A Low Temple

A low temple keeps its gods in the dark.
You lend a matchbox to the priest.
One by one the gods come to light.
Amused bronze. Smiling stone. Unsurprised.
For a moment the length of a matchstick
gesture after gesture revives and dies.
Stance after lost stance is found
and lost again.
Who was that, you ask.
The eight arm goddess, the priest replies.
A sceptic match coughs.
You can count.
But she has eighteen, you protest.
All the same she is still an eight arm goddess to the priest.
You come out in the sun and light a charminar.
Children play on the back of the twenty foot tortoise.

The Pattern

a checkerboard pattern
some old men must have drawn
yesterday

with a piece of chalk
on the back of the twenty foot
tortoise

smudges under the bare feet
and gets fainter all the time as
the children run

The Horseshoe Shrine

That nick in the rock
is really a kick in the side of the hill.
It's where a hoof
struck

like a thunderbolt
when Khandoba
with the bride sidesaddle behind him on the blue
horse

jumped across the valley
and the three
went on from there like one
spark

fleeing from flint.
To a home that waited
on the other side of the hill like a hay
stack.

Manohar

The door was open.
Manohar thought
it was one more temple.

He looked inside.
Wondering
which god he was going to find.

He quickly turned away
when a wide eyed calf
looked back at him.

It isn't another temple,
he said,
it's just a cowshed.

Chaitanya

sweet as grapes
are the stones of jejuri
said chaitanya

he popped a stone
in his mouth
and spat out gods

The Butterfly

There is no story behind it.
It is split like a second.
It hinges around itself.

It has no future.
It is pinned down to no past.
It's a pun on the present.

It's a little yellow butterfly.
It has taken these wretched hills
under its wings.

Just a pinch of yellow,
it opens before it closes
and closes before it o

where is it

A Scratch

what is god
and what is stone
the dividing line
if it exists
is very thin
at jejuri
and every other stone
is god or his cousin

there is no crop
other than god
and god is harvested here
around the year
and round the clock
out of the bad earth
and the hard rock

that giant hunk of rock
the size of a bedroom
is khandoba's wife turned to stone
the crack that runs right across

67

is the scar from his broadsword
he struck her down with
once in a fit of rage

scratch a rock
and a legend springs

Ajamil and the Tigers

The tiger people went to their king
and said, 'We're starving.
We've had nothing to eat,
not a bite,
for 15 days and 16 nights.
Ajamil has got
a new sheep dog.
He cramps our style
and won't let us get within a mile
of meat.'

'That's shocking,'
said the tiger king.
'Why didn't you come to see me before?
Make preparations for a banquet.
I'm gonna teach that sheep dog a lesson he'll never forget.'
'Hear hear', said the tigers.
'Careful,' said the queen.
But he was already gone.
Alone
into the darkness before the dawn.

In an hour he was back,
the good king.
A black patch on his eye.
His tail in a sling.
And said, 'I've got it all planned
now that I know the lie of the land.

68

All of us will have to try.
We'll outnumber the son of a bitch.
And this time there will be no hitch.
Because this time I shall be leading the attack.'

Quick as lightning
the sheep dog was.
He took them all in as prisoners of war,
the 50 tigers and the tiger king,
before they could get their paws
on a single sheep.
They never had a chance.
The dog was in 51 places all at once.
He strung them all out in a daisy chain
and flung them in front of his boss in one big heap.

'Nice dog you got there, Ajamil,'
said the tiger king.
Looking a little ill
and spitting out a tooth.
'But there's been a bit of a misunderstanding.
We could've wiped out your herd in one clean sweep.
But we were not trying to creep up on your sheep.
We feel that means are more important than ends.
We were coming to see you as friends.
And that's the truth.'

The sheep dog was the type
who had never told a lie in his life.
He was built along simpler lines
and he was simply disgusted.
He kept on making frantic signs.
But Ajamil, the good shepherd
refused to meet his eyes
and pretended to believe every single word
of what the tiger king said.
And seemed to be taken in by all the lies.

Ajamil cut them loose
and asked them all to stay for dinner.
It was an offer the tigers couldn't refuse.
And after the lamb chops and the roast,
when Ajamil proposed
they sign a long term friendship treaty,
all the tigers roared,
'We couldn't agree with you more.'
And swore they would be good friends all their lives
as they put down the forks and the knives.

Ajamil signed a pact
with the tiger people and sent them back.
Laden with gifts of sheep, leather jackets and balls of wool.
Ajamil wasn't a fool.
Like all good shepherds he knew
that even tigers have got to eat some time.
A good shepherd sees to it they do.
He is free to play a flute all day
as well fed tigers and fat sheep drink from the same pond
with a full stomach for a common bond.

Chaitanya

a herd of legends
on a hill slope
looked up from its grazing
when chaitanya came in sight

the hills remained still
when chaitanya
was passing by
a cowbell tinkled
when he disappeared from view
and the herd of legends
returned to its grazing

Between Jejuri and the Railway Station

You leave the little temple town
with its sixty three priests inside their sixty three houses
huddled at the foot of the hill
with its three hundred pillars, five hundred steps and eighteen arches.
You pass the sixty fourth house of the temple dancer
who owes her prosperity to another skill.
A skill the priest's son would rather not talk about.
A house he has never stepped inside
and hopes he never will.
ou pass by the ruin of the temple but the resident bitch is nowhere around.
You pass by the Gorakshanath Hair Cutting Saloon.
You pass by the Mhalasakant Cafe
and the flour mill.
And that's it.
The end.
You've left the town behind
with a coconut in your hand,
a priest's visiting card in your pocket
and a few questions knocking about in your head.
You stop halfway between
Jejuri on the one and the railway station on the other hand.
You stop dead
and stand still like a needle in a trance.
Like a needle that has struck a perfect balance between equal scales
with nothing left to add or shed.
What has stopped you in your tracks
and taken your breath away
is the sight
of a dozen cocks and hens in a field of jowar
in a kind of a harvest dance. The craziest you've ever seen.

Where seven jump straight up to at least four times their height
as five come down with grain in their beaks.

```
                            a
              n            n              n           p        &
up           a  d      do  w          d           u
              d          u        do
      &     wo       a    p      a  d    w    &        u
              n                   n          n                   p
              d
a                         o                      d         n
n    u      an         w    &    u     an    do      a d      u
d    p      d          n              p              n
d                 n  d               d               a
o    &  u        a       d w        n    u        a    n      o wn   &
w       p               o  n    a        u        n       d       &
n                                        d
                p                                 w
              u          a  n     u  p       d o  n      a         a  n
an  d         d  n            n       d         n           d         u
```

And there you stand forgetting how silly you must look
with a priest on your left shoulder as it were
and a station master on your right.

The Railway Station

1 : the indicator

a wooden saint
in need of paint

the indicator
has turned inward
ten times over

72

swallowed the names
of all the railway
stations it knows

removed its hands
from its face
and put them away
in its pockets

if it knows when
the next train's due
it gives no clue

the clockface adds
its numerals

the total is zero

2 : the station dog

the spirit of the place
lives inside the mangy body
of the station dog

doing penance for the last
three hundred years under
the tree of arrivals and departures

the dog opens his right eye
just long enough to look at you and see
whether you're a man a demon a demigod

or the eight armed railway timetable come
to stroke him on the head
with a healing hand

and to take him to heaven
the dog decides
that day is not yet

73

3 : the tea stall

the young novice at the tea stall
has taken a vow of silence

when you ask him a question
he exorcises you

by sprinkling dishwater in your face
and continues with his ablutions in the sink

and certain ceremonies connected
with the washing of cups and saucers

4 : the station master

the booking clerk believes in the doctrine
of the next train
when conversation turns to time
he takes his tongue
hands it to you across the counter
and directs you to a superior
intelligence

the two headed station master
belongs to a sect
that rejects every timetable
not published in the year the track was laid
as apocryphal
but interprets the first timetable
with a freedom that allows him to read
every subsequent timetable between
the lines of its text

he keeps looking anxiously at the setting sun
as if the sunset were a part of a secret ritual
and he didn't want anything to go wrong with it
at the last minute

finally he nods like a stroke
between a yes and a no
and says
all timetables ever published
along with all timetables yet to be published
are simultaneously valid
at any given time and on any given track
insofar as all the timetables were inherent
in the one printed
when the track was laid

and goes red
in both his faces
at once

5 : vows

slaughter a goat before the clock
smash a coconut on the railway track
smear the indicator with the blood of a cock
bathe the station master in milk
and promise you will give
a solid gold toy train to the booking clerk
if only someone would tell you
when the next train is due

6 : the setting sun

the setting sun
touches upon the horizon
at a point where the rails
like the parallels
of a prophecy
appear to meet

the setting sun
large as a wheel

75

Keki N. Daruwalla

Keki Nasserwanji Daruwalla was born in Lahore in 1937 and educated at Government College, Ludhiana. He lives in New Delhi and works for the Government of India. Daruwalla's volumes of poetry are *Under Orion* (1970), *Apparition in April* (1971), *Crossing of Rivers* (1976), *Winter Poems* (1980), *The Keeper of the Dead* (1982)—winner of the Sahitya Akademi Award of 1984—and *Landscapes* (1987). He has also published *Sword and Abyss* (1979), a collection of short stories, and edited *Two Decades of Indian Poetry: 1960–1980* (1980).

When *Keynote* magazine asked him to comment on any one of his poems, Daruwalla chose 'The King Speaks to the Scribe'. 'I acquired my love for the dramatic monologue from Robert Browning,' he wrote, and described its subject, Asoka, as 'a favourite king ... [whose] change of heart following the battle of Kalinga is one of the greatest dramatic moments in history.' He concludes:

> I consider this one of my most significant poems because the language of the edicts merges into it without jarring. I have tried to bring out the passion and the quiet dignity of the man and yet avoid pomposity. Incidentally, the words juxtaposed in the poem are from the Thirteenth Edict ...
>
> For me, one of the most satisfying aspects of the poem is its rhythm (iambic pentameter) and its clarity. The character of the speaker also changes. Though denying humility in the beginning, he sinks into it in the end.
>
> Finally, a poem is a child, you like it in its totality, and not because of a line here or a limb there.[1]

An earlier statement of his, though more general, gives an organically different view of the poem, seeing it as an empty mug perhaps, into which you pour the liquid of your choice:

> It is unfashionable to say so, but I feel even in poetry content is more important than form. For me poetry is first personal—exploratory, at times therapeutic. ... At the same time it has to be

---

[1] 'Drawing on History', *Keynote* (Bombay), No. 2 (April 1982), 55.

a social gesture, because on occasions I feel external reality bearing down on me from all sides with a pressure strong enough to tear the ear-drums. My poems are rooted in landscape . . . [It] is not merely there to set the scene but to lead to an illumination. It should be the eye of the spiral . . . For me a riot-stricken town is landscape.[2]

And indeed it is with just such a landscape that Daruwalla opens his first book.

> Blood and fog
> are over half the town
> and curfew stamps along the empty street
> ('Curfew—In a Riot-Torn-City')

However much external reality may have damaged the poet's ear-drums, it has, at least here, left the part sensitive to verse pattern intact. The pattern, a cretic followed by two iambic lines, seems to have come of its own, instinctively; also, the third line's alternating monosyllabic and disyllabic words follow the very pace of weary soldiers marching through empty streets. But Daruwalla, who is more prospector than goldsmith, is not always so lucky. He slips into poeticisms ('The storm came ere he could / map the country') and clichés ('at last, the sun comes out / the well-fleshed face of a Persian girl / emerging from diaphanous veils') even in his latest book, *Landscapes*, and if he has his moments of vision, he also has those of clumsiness ('I present them: / my brown-loaf face'), so much so that at least one critic has suggested that Daruwalla do some hard thinking.

Much of Daruwalla's early poetry is concerned with things tele-printers are busy with: floods, famines, riots, and anniversaries. That the news is delivered in verse should make all the difference, but seldom does. A later sequence is titled 'Vignette', and it is just that; another picks up 'the old slave-route of the Hindu psyche'. He has travel poems from which the sense of place is missing, and narratives that, rightly, hinge on details of local history. He has interminable love poems. But there are poems, too, like 'Wolf', where instead of pursuing his subject through mixed metaphors and mixed rhythms, he releases it—in himself:

[2] Keki N. Daruwalla, ed., *Two Decades of Indian Poetry: 1960–1980*, New Delhi, 1980, 21.

Black snout on sulphur body
he nudged his way
into my consciousness.

This inward movement and outward thrust, a process that im-
plicates both heart and bone, the human body *tout court*, in the crime
of writing, is worked out in 'The Unrest of Desire':

However you bury the shadow in the heart
under slabs of concrete and a coil of bone,
however you wall the cave-impulse at the mouth,
it will hammer at the sides and break free . . .

When it does break free, the lines have the temperature of molten
rock; cooling, they form stanzas:

I saw the wild hawk-king this morning
riding an ascending wind
as he drilled the sky.
The land beneath him was filmed with salt:
grass-seed, insect, bird—
nothing could thrive here. But he was lost
in the momentum of his own gyre,
a frustrated parricide on the kill.
The fuse of his hate was burning still.

('Hawk')

It is difficult to keep to the third person under such pressure, and the
last section of 'Hawk' is in monologue. The poem reads like a com-
panion piece to Ted Hughes's famous one on the same bird and is
just as striking, their closures equally strong and absolute:

. . . and it will rain hawks.

(Daruwalla)

I am going to keep things like this.

(Hughes)

'It is the victor he loves, not war. He thrills to strength with all the
envy, the trembling, of a mortal man.'[3] One would think this was
said of Daruwalla; in fact it is Calvin Bedient on Hughes. As for the
victims, they don't stand a chance anyway. In 'Hawk', what chance

[3] Calvin Bedient, *Eight Contemporary Poets*, London, Oxford University Press,
1974, 101.

does the luckless hare have against 'the squall of wings above'? And what chance the young revolutionary in his prison cell?

> . . . a shadow
> that fell tree-like across his cell,
> was that the angel of death
> or a lawyer wringing his hands
> pleading for bail?
>> ('The Revolutionary')

The writing, whether of hawks or men, from the frontlines of ancient history or from those more recent, returns to the same bleak truism again and again: an axe head lashed to a handle is no match for 'a copper axe with a shaft-hole'. 'Why do they stuff history with dates and battle-orders?' he asks in 'A City Falls'. 'Why not show flowers, crosses, candles and leave it there?' The nameless twentieth-century city of the poem is as much Mohenjo Daro as New Delhi, and in the narrow space between those dates and that flower, Daruwalla puts down his abundant lines.

Hawk

1

I saw the wild hawk-king this morning
riding an ascending wind
as he drilled the sky.
The land beneath him was filmed with salt:
grass-seed, insect, bird—
nothing could thrive here. But he was lost
in the momentum of his own gyre,
a frustrated parricide on the kill.
The fuse of his hate was burning still.

But in the evening he hovered above
the groves, a speck of barbed passion.
Crow, mynah and pigeon roosted here
while parakeets flew raucously by.
And then he ran amok,
a rapist in the harem of the sky.
As he went up with a pigeon
skewered to his heel-talon
he scanned the other birds, marking out their fate,
the ones he would scoop up next,
those black dregs in the cup of his hate!

2

The tamed one is worse, for he is touched by man.
When snared in the woods
his eyelids are sewn with silk
as he is broken to the hood.
He is momentarily blinded, starved.
Then the scar over his vision is perforated.
Morsels of vision are fed to his eyes
as he is unblinded stitch by relenting stitch.
Slowly the world re-forms:
mud walls, trees burgeon.
His eye travels like the eye of the storm.

Discovering his eye
and the earth and sky
with it, he leaps from earth to ether.
Now the sky is his eyrie.
He ferocious floats on splayed wings;
then plummets like a flare,
smoking, and a gust of feathers
proclaims that he has struck.
The tamed one is worse, for he is touched by man.
Hawking is turned to a ritual, the predator's
passion honed to an art;
as they feed the hawk by carving the breast
of the quarry bird and gouging out his heart.

3

They have flushed him out of the tall grasses,
the hare, hunted now
in pairs by mother hawk and son.
They can't kill him in one fell swoop.
But each time the talons cart away
a patch of ripped fur.
He diminishes, one talon-morsel at a time.
He is stunned by the squall of wings above.
His heart is a burning stable
packed with whinnying horses.
His blood writes stories on the scuffed grass!
His movements are a scribble on the page of death.

4

I wouldn't know when I was stolen from the eyrie
I can't remember when I was ensnared.
I only know the leather disc
which blots out the world
and the eyelids which burn with thwarted vision.

Then the perforations, and yet
the blue iris of heaven does not come through.
I can think of a patch of blue sky

when shown a blue slide.
But I am learning how to spot the ones
crying for the right to dream, the right to flesh,
the right to sleep with their own wives—
I have placed them. I am sniffing
the air currents, deciding when to pounce.

I will hover like a black prophecy
weaving its moth-soft cocoon of death.
I shall drive down
with the compulsive thrust of gravity,
trained for havoc,
my eyes focused on them
like the sights of a gun.

During the big drought which is surely going to come
the doves will look up for clouds, and it will rain hawks.

The King Speaks to the Scribe

(Third century B.C.)

First Kartikeya, there's no pride involved,
nor humility; understand this. I speak
of atonement, that is, if blood can ever
be wiped away with words. We will engrave
this message on volcanic rock, right here
where the earth still reeks of slaughter.
A hundred thousand courted death, mind you.
The battlefield stank so that heaven
had to hold a cloth to its nose. I trod
this plain, dark and glutinous with gore,
my chariot-wheels squelching in the bloody mire.

Nothing stands now between them and destruction,
neither moat nor bridge nor hut nor door-leaf.
No lighted tapers call them to their village.

It is to them that you will speak, or rather
I will speak through you. So don't enunciate
the law of piety, no aphorisms
which say that good is difficult and sin easy.
And no palaver about two peafowl
and just one antelope roasting in my kitchen
instead of an entire hecatomb as in
my father's days. There may be huts where
they have nothing to burn on the hearth-fires.
Spare me the shame. And no taboos, please,
forbidding the caponing of roosters
or drinking of spirituous liquors,
the castration of bulls and rams and
the branding of horses. So listen with care,
Kartikeya, and I will tell you what to write.
First talk about the sorrows of conquest
and other miseries attendant on
enslavement. In all lands live Brahmins,
anchorites and householders, each enmeshed
in the outer skin of relationships,
that network of duty and herd impulse
through which each charts his particular furrow.
And the sword falls on such people and their
children are blighted, while the affection
of their friends remains undiminished.
Mark that, don't talk merely of rapine and slaughter
but also of separation from loved ones.

And about my sorrow what will you say?
How will you touch that weed-ridden lake-floor
of my despair and keep from drowning?
Say simply that of all the people killed
or captured, if the thousandth part were to
suffer as before, the pain would overwhelm me.
Tell them I have abjured pride, the lowest
can abuse me now and I shall not answer.
Let the dust of humility cover my head.
Even the tribals, dark and bullet-headed,
the blubber-skinned, the ones from whom our demons

and *yakshas* have borrowed their faces,
I invite to my fold. Let them turn from crime
and their aboriginal ways and they will not suffer.

Cut deeper than the cuts of my sword
so that even as moss covers the letters
they are visible. Write whatever
you chance on. Don't look for a white-quartz boulder.
Anything will do, a mass of trap rock
or just a stone sheet. And the language simple,
something the forest folk can understand.
I am not speaking to kings, to Antiyoka
and Maga or Alikasudra. And no
high-flown language. I am not here
to appease gods. Even they must be ignored
for a while and their altar-fires turn cold.
Men don't have enough fuel to burn their dead.

Mind you, Kartikeya, between me and them is blood.
Your words will have to reach across to them
like a tide of black oxen crossing a ford.

The Unrest of Desire

The unrest of desire is lit up with eyes.
Whatever mask you slap upon your face,
however you tear at the soft throat of life
and probe the salt-blood with your insistent tongue
the unrest of desire is revealed by eyes.

However you bury the shadow in the heart
under slabs of concrete and a coil of bone,
however you wall the cave-impulse at the mouth,
it will hammer at the sides and break free,
however you bury the shadow in the heart.

You may etch the shadow on the cavern-wall
and turn your drives into aborigine art:
bison and stag loping in charcoal lines.
You can't erase the burn. It will char your dreams
however you bury the shadow in the heart.

Wolf

Fire-lit
half silhouette and half myth
the wolf circles my past
treading the leaves into a bed
till he sleeps, black snout
on extended paws.

Black snout on sulphur body
he nudged his way
into my consciousness.
Prowler, wind-sniffer, throat-catcher,
his cries drew a ring
around my night;
a child's night is a village
on the forest edge.

My mother said
his ears stand up
at the fall of dew
he can sense a shadow
move across a hedge
on a dark night;
he can sniff out
your approaching dreams;
there is nothing
that won't be lit up
by the dark torch of his eyes.

The wolves have been slaughtered now.
A hedge of smoking gun-barrels
rings my daughter's dreams.

Fish are Speared by Night

Fish are netted by day here
        speared by night.
A tongue of coral protrudes under the tide
where the men stand loin-deep
in foam, their black-basalt legs
braced against the surf, legs like
an outcrop of the reef itself, so still
that moss moves towards it, impelled
by some primeval instinct of its own.

Flashlights stab the sea;
from shoulder-height javelins descend,
splintering the light as the fish is skewered
and forced down the spear-head,
still threshing the sand.

At the thatch village two hours before dawn
dogs bark tentatively and silhouette-wives
receive them with hurricane-lanterns—
the men with their harvest on their backs,
shell-grit and sand still clinging to their feet.

But when clouds go about like shrieking gulls
and each wave descends from its cliff-top
like a cataract, and the wicker-lamps are snuffed out,
they spread their fishing-nets on the ground
and spread their women over them
        splay-legged.
Fish here are speared by night.

Chinar

The chinar confronts the sunset
with its own dusk.
You can hear the drip of crinkled leaf.
Isn't this what they call dry rain,
this slow, twisting dead-moth descent
from the sapless branch?

In the eye of the lake
and the running eye of Jhelum
it holds you, this bonfire death
that slowly drips fire,
these smouldering rusts
without the clank of metal.
A wind alights on the tree
and the eye cannot follow
each bronze-scale severed
from the mail of the dying giant,
each clenched child-fist of a leaf,
the largesse of it
the aching drift of it
the flame and the fall of it.

Night Fishing

A shorelamp drops
its lighted tackle.
On the hook
no fish-snout spin.
Night fishing
sad as night rain
alone as the mind
before the dreams crowd in.

Dom Moraes

Dominic Frank Moraes was born in Bombay in 1938, and educated there and at Jesus College, Oxford, where he read English. His first book of poems, *A Beginning* (1957), published when he was only nineteen, won the Hawthornden Prize in 1958. He has since published *Poems* (1960), *John Nobody* (1965), *Poems 1955–1965* (1966), *Beldam & Others* (1967), *Collected Poems 1957–1987* (1987), and *Serendip* (1990). *Absences* appeared in a privately printed limited edition in 1983. *The Brass Serpent* (1964) is a volume of translations from the Hebrew of T. Carmi. Moraes has also written twenty-three books of prose. These include biographies, travelogues, and collections of reportage, but except for his autobiography, *My Son's Father* (1968), few seem likely to be remembered. Moraes's journalistic assignments have taken him to most countries in the world, and for the past decade he has lived in Bombay.

Moraes's burden, especially in his early poetry, is dispossession: the loss, on growing up, of boyhood visions. Whereas most people accept this as the price of growing up and don't give it a second thought, Moraes, with the stubbornness of a child, keeps running back to his imaginary kingdom:

> That dream, her eyes like rock studded the high
> Mountain of her body that I was to climb.
>
> ('Snow on a Mountain')

> This man, awash in sleep, had tossed all night,
> Dreaming that in a meadow rough with stubble
> Some strangers with long cloaks had come in sight:
> Angels, who showed no trace of human trouble.
>
> ('A Man Dreaming')

> Nightly when foxes walk,
> Owls fly, rats shriek, they wake,
> Through closed eyes, to islands
> Furled in a blue silence
> Where the brushed sun is docile
> And the flushed mothers smile

88

And the tall fathers stay at home all day
And nobody can die.

('The Children')

The first two quotations are from *A Beginning*, the earliest poem of which was written when Moraes was sixteen; the last is from *John Nobody*, published when he was twenty-seven. I don't think there's been another poet who dawdled this long in so wishful a landscape.

For the next seventeen years Moraes wrote little poetry: he had, he said, 'come to a dead end', and though 'still trying to write . . . failed to produce anything good.' He says looking back on this time,

> I prefer to think of it as a germination period for words, while experience and travel took over my life. In 1982, I began once more to write well enough to satisfy myself. One theme I followed derived from the early books, where I had an image of a lost but compulsive dancer, who is followed by a young man who hopes to return from following him with wisdom. When the young man returns, nobody will listen to him, 'Because you are ugly and no longer young' [see 'Words to a Boy' below]. Several of my new poems were written from the point of view of the young man after his return. I also tried to avoid the personal pronoun, which I had not done in my early work, and to identify myself with historical or mythological characters with whom I felt I had something in common. I visualised the unhappiness and emptiness, not of myself, but of a shattered world.[1]

Jason, Sinbad, and Babur are a few of the characters Moraes identifies with. Like all masks, these, too, occasionally fuse with the wearer's skin:

My crew and I were beardless boys
But driven by a mystery.

('Jason')

Ashes and marred walls deface you.
Where is this wind from,
Sinbad, defining its own course?
Some of us never know home.

('Sinbad')

---

[1] 'Time and the Poet', *Debonair* (Bombay), October 1989, 61.

The dead in the dust.
Familiars of the field, vultures
Alate as angels on each corpse.
One, in that sleeping, seemed my son.
With a great cry I drove them away,
Awoke weeping, ate opium confection:
Drowsy afterwards, saw myself
As I am, lonely in all lands.

('Babur')

It is important to remember, though, that Moraes can strike this wandering note even without the historical/mythological disguise, as in the poem addressed to his Oxford contemporary Peter Levi:

Then you went home, all of you went home.
To high tea, Gentleman's Relish, maturity.
At the end all of you knew where you came from.

All of you now have homes, Peter, not me.

('For Peter')

Here homelessness is much more than a metaphor for exile. The feeling may not be expressed in so many words, but Moraes's dislocation from two literatures, Indian and English, is indicated on at least one other occasion:

Geoffrey, goodbye: four rows of shelves
Separate Hill from Moraes.
We shall have to be borrowed and stamped
And put back in the wrong places
If we are ever to meet.

('Interludes VII')

'You're in a peculiar historical position, you know', the anthropologist Verrier Elwin was to tell Dom Moraes, then aged eighteen.

All your family speak English, and, really, you yourself are a very English person. Your reactions aren't Indian, are they? I can't explain that, but there it is. You seem quite naturally to live in a world of English poetry and English painting, and you are an English poet.[2]

[2] *My Son's Father: An Autobiography*, 1968; rpt., New Delhi, 1990, 164.

For nearly three decades Moraes's readers, too, saw him as an 'English poet', and even though this has now changed, the foreignness of his verse has not gone away, nor can it, nor would he want it to.

Writing to his mother from England—'this cold, tidy country'—he says,

> Your dream is desolate.
> It calls me every day
> But I cannot enter it.
> You know I will not return.
> Forgive me my trespasses.
>
> ('Letter to my Mother')

In 1974 Moraes returned to 'Where seven islands squat / In a filthy sea', and in a recent poem feels sufficiently distanced from his old wintry self—'The great dishevelled world of my distress'—to write of it in the third person:

> Perhaps he is wholly changed:
> But his attire, quartz armour,
> Acquired in winter courts,
> Shelters him from our summer.
>
> ('Exile')

But has he 'wholly changed'? Not if by 'change' is meant that 'his rhymes and pictures' have become closer to our seasons than they were before. Instead, the distance seems to have given him psychological space, room for manoeuvre, almost a new location, and the result has been a series of quite magnificent love poems, transparent as quartz, and filled with sensuousness, which is its own peace:

> Time will not stop: and you are very tired.
> Turn into my arms and truly sleep.
> Turn into my arms and be desired.
>
> The deep hurt in you like the sun disturbs
> My dawns: but sometimes you are still in sleep,
> Smelling of armpits and of wet herbs.
>
> ('Asleep')

DOM MORAES

Autobiography

A child, the soft-pawed sky held up my kites.
Tumultuous images rose from the mud.
My eyes like fish flickered through sunken lights
Under the poems dancing in my blood.
And from this great, this all-gate-breaking flood,
My thoughts like pincers lifted tastes and sights.
My heart delved down to love, knowledge of God,
Waited the king in sandals on the heights.

But even then I was as cold as stone,
Sinking among the ripples of the crowd,
And now all my desire is to atone
For an unfriendly springtime, webbed in cloud.
I remember my grandmother, crescent-browed,
Falling from Time, leaf-light, too much alone:
And my grandfather, who was small and proud.
Tumult of images, where have you gone?

The ageing chemist in his drawing room, terse,
Gentle: the sea like soapsuds in the night,
Seen from a ship: the moon, leprous, inverse,
Rising: the girl at Hanoi with her white
Hands and dog's eyes, dripping with amber light:
Have these things shaped me for the craft of verse?
Do they remain, giving a sad insight?
And have I changed for better or for worse?

I have grown up, I think, to live alone,
To keep my old illusions, sometimes dream
Glumly that I am unloved and forlorn,
Run away from strangers, often seem
Unreal to myself in the pulpy warmth of a sunbeam.
I have grown up, hand on the primal bone,
Making the poem, taking the word from the stream,
Fighting the sand for speech, fighting the stone.

DOM MORAES

Words to a Boy

I cannot speak to you. Our chances
Lessen each day, I think, but you must still
Follow the lonely dancer when he dances
Over the shoulder of the farthest hill
Where boulders lie. Which king advances

Through the tumultuous plains, or what retreat
Is made through marshes, you know nothing of.
Only the scuffed grass and the dancer's feet
Can your eyes understand, for too much love
Affects the eyes, makes vision incomplete.

So you one day will lose the dancer.
He will cry out and fall, he will have passed
Beyond your questions to the place of answer,
The final solitude, to find at last
Stillness of rocks and tumult of the past.

Return, with lifted hands and prophet's tongue.
Your people will not see your vision,
For they sleep under the dark angel's wing.
When you cry out to them they will not listen
Because you are ugly and no longer young.

Two from Israel

I. RENDEZVOUS
(for Nathan Altermann)

Altermann, sipping wine, reads with a look
Of infinite patience and slight suffering.
When I approach him, he puts down his book,

Waves to the chair beside him like a king,
Then claps his hands, and an awed waiter fetches
Bread, kosher sausage, cake, a chicken's wing,

93

More wine, some English cigarettes, and matches.
'Eat, eat,' Altermann says, 'this is good food.'
Through the awning over us the sunlight catches

His aquiline sad head, till it seems hewed
From tombstone marble. I accept some bread.
I've lunched already, but would not seem rude.

When I refuse more, he feeds me instead,
Heaping my plate, clapping for wine, his eyes
—Expressionless inside the marble head—

Appearing not to notice how the flies
Form a black, sticky icing on the cake.
Thinking of my health now, I visualise

The Aryan snow floating, flake upon flake,
Over the ghetto wall where only fleas
Fed well, and they and hunger kept awake

Under sharp stars, those waiting for release.
Birds had their nests, but Jews nowhere to hide
When visited by vans and black police.

The shekinah rose where a people died,
A pillar of flame by night, of smoke by day.
From Europe then the starved and terrified

Flew. Now their mourner sits in this café,
Telling me how to scan a Hebrew line.
Though my attention has moved far away

His features stay marble and aquiline.
But the eternal gesture of his race
Flowing through the hands that offer bread and wine

Reveals the deep love sealed in the still face.

94

DOM MORAES

II. *SPREE*
(for Yosl Bergner)

Tonight I see your blue protuberant eyes
Following your angry wife, who sweeps away,
With their perpetual look of mild surprise.

'*Nu*, have another drink for luck,' you say.
I settle back to let your swift talk flow
Freer with drink through the small hours till day

Reddens the bottles in your studio,
While, still unchecked, a rapid spate of words
Explains some brush technique I did not know.

A Polish boy, you took cadaverous birds,
Perched in a burnt-out Europe, for your text,
Then came here, but kept sympathy towards

Creatures with wings, for you chose angels next,
Though different from those flaming ones that flew
Into the Bible: yours are too perplexed

Even to fly, waifs without work to do.
Yudl reproved you once, in the Cassit:
'Your angels are not Israelis, Jew.'

No: but they are the images we meet
In every mirror: so I understand
Those helpless angels waiting in the street

For somebody to take them by the hand.
Still, hangovers won't wait, so now we walk
Past herons down the beach towards liquor land.

There's not much left to talk of: but you talk,
Waving both arms, eccentric, Yiddish, free,
In your new land where tall winged creatures stalk

Between the hostile mountains and the sea.

95

8

Prophet

I followed desert suns
Alone, these thirty years,
A goatskin knotted round my sex,
My fodder what I found,
My shelter under rocks,
My visions in my eye
That mapped the slow wind flowing
Across the sunwashed dunes, or the
Scuffed dwarf spoor of the ant.
Once these kept me happy.

Tufted with tamarisk
The tawny dunes end
Suddenly in shadow.
The ridged rocks rise.
The known desolate land
Kisses my bare feet.
Infested by winged things
The rough hair of the sky
Teems in the sun's eye.
Kindling the dunes, the enraged
Wind beats up sand. The awkward ant
Gnaws in a dry pasture.

I have aged.

Key

Ground in the Victorian lock, stiff,
With difficulty screwed open,
To admit me to the seven mossed stairs
And the badly kept garden.

Who runs to me in memory
Through flowers destroyed by no love

But the child with brown hair and eyes,
Smudged all over with toffee?

I lick his cheeks. I bounce him in air.
Two bounces, he disappears.

Fifteen years later, he redescends,
Not as a postponed child, but a letter
Asking me for his father who now possesses
No garden, no home, not even any key.

from *Interludes*

VII

LIBRARY
(*For Geoffrey Hill*)

The twigs of my fingers
Shake leafwords down: sound
Of dust falling on silk,
Dust falling on marble
Busts in the library where
We shall finally be embedded:
The hospital for dead poets.

We shall have healed into books
Maybe not read by too many.

Geoffrey, goodbye: four rows of shelves
Separate Hill from Moraes.
We shall have to be borrowed and stamped
And put back in the wrong places
If we are ever to meet.

Sinbad

Winds sniffed, the graves
Of each sea identified,
Numbered, still the tickled waves
Fumbling, toss off the dead.

Sinbad, your trips!
Diamonds clawed by vultures!
Flying over defunct countries
You need raw colours for new maps.

Old friends folding up in strange places.
New friends holding out hearts.
Bronze breasts iced in white lace:
Cold cups of kindness.

Choose your rock, seamate, stay with it.
Lose your shadow, it's of no use.
The last bronze bird puts you down,
Tidier than a horse, final.

Ashes and marred walls deface you.
Where is this wind from,
Sinbad, defining its own course?
Some of us never know home.

from *Steles*

I

The word works. The world doesn't.
Oases dehydrate. The word
Moves where the sirocco hasn't.
Put one word on my stele.

No need for effusion.
The words are firmly placed.
The worlds are words pressed
Together, like firm breasts.

Fewer words live than two.
One should bring them down to one
To spring from silk to the mind,
Free, buoyant, beautiful.

Sip it at the tip. It answers.
The word provides milk:
The one word dancing always
Towards desert horizons.

IV

What is this airdrift from Chile
And murdered Allende, to freeze me?
Whose is the figure in the mind,
Caped and demanding entry?

The worlds and words build and build
In temples in a rainy country.
Dead gods wait by the Amazon
For my eventual arrivals.

The thing in my mind takes off its cape.
Underneath is a black lace brassière
And huge breasts, but a condor's head,
Yellow eyes on the endless Andes.

Breakfast, the papers are here.
Claws scrape the sill.
Condors, beaked riders of wind,
Shriek on my stele.

VI

On my stele, mark colours,
Appraisals of sound and wind,
The scented flesh of my wife,
A Siamese cat, a dachshund.

And me, unsteady of mind,
Departing between these textures
With knowledge of worlds, winds,
Lipstick, scent, flesh, fur.

Who will paint this stele?
It will have more colours than white,
Red on black vases, yellow roses,
Turquoise water, or the changing light.

From far away I watch
Sound and wind take shape.
Lipstick touches my cheek
Before exhausted sleep.

VII

She in her youth arose,
Shape moulded by mild winds:
Hips to launch many ships,
Nippled bowls of cream and honey,

Face never to be forgotten,
Odour of thyme and wild roses.
Bad poets swooned at her feet
With bouquets of dead sonnets.

Now tourists and crows visit her,
Braving the dust and the dusk.
Her light feet rustled the leaves,
Not knowing they moved among mysteries.

Drying crowshit and snails mar
The symmetry of her stele.
Red worms have stripped her bare
To squirm under skeletons.

VIII

Time and the river, aflame
With the explosion of suns,
Swept mysteries and monsters inshore.
Cyclops drank in my cellars.

Slowly shifted round, the ground plates
Of earth underfoot, I kept balance.
Pterodactyls nested in my chimneys,
Birds made of leather.

Salamander, the word of fire,
Dragged from its element, gaffed,
Writhed between death and stele
As time and the river turned to ash.

The cyclops died of alcohol.
Oxygen killed the others.
But the salamander endured,
The mystery beyond the monsters.

X

Floes creak out of the north,
Glided over by birds:
Foes no fire can unfreeze,
Guarded by white bears.

Proserpine, lady of spring,
Does not guard or guide us.
Where is she in this winter?
How shall we hide from the snow,

Heavy on our breaking roofs,
In our beating hearts
Taken by a cold hand?
Darkness, the smell of unknown seas.

Have we time to inscribe our steles?
And who will read them?
Whose are these great caped figures
Coming down, silent, from the floes?

Future Plans

Absorbed with each other's flesh
In the tumbled beds of our youth,
We had conversations with children
Not born to us yet, but named.
Those faculties, now disrupted,
Shed selves, must exist somewhere,
As they did when our summer ended:
Leela-Claire, and the first death.
Mark, cold on a hospital tray
At five months: I was away then
With tribesmen in bronze forests.
We became our children, my wife.
Now, left alone with each other,
As we were in four continents,
At the turn of your classic head,
At your private smile, the beacon
You beckon with, I recall them.
We may travel there once more.
We shall leave at the proper time,
As a couple, without complaint,
With a destination in common
And some regrets and memories.
We shall leave in ways we believed
Impossible in our youth,
A little tired, but in the end,
Not unhappy to have lived.

Dilip Chitre

Dilip Purushottam Chitre was born in Baroda in 1938, and grew up there and in Bombay. After taking a B.A. (Hons.) degree in English from Bombay University in 1959, he went to Ethiopia for three years to teach in schools. In the late sixties and seventies he was associated with the magazine *Quest* (now *New Quest*), for which he wrote essays, reviews, and a regular column of comment. His first book of poems in Marathi, *Kavita*, appeared in 1960, and his second in 1978. He has also published a book of short stories, a travelogue, and a collection of critical essays in Marathi, and edited *An Anthology of Marathi Poetry: 1945–1965* (1967), doing most of the translations himself. For the past three decades, Chitre's work-in-progress has been a translation of the Marathi saint-poet Tukaram, a part of which is now published in *Says Tuka* (1991). *Travelling in a Cage* (1980) is Chitre's only collection in English so far, and represents just a fraction of his English poems. However, it includes *Ambulance Ride* (1972), a long poem that appeared privately.

The romantic theory that bound the writer to his native speech and language to a specific people no longer rings true. In a lecture delivered at Bombay University in 1989, Chitre spoke instead of bilingual traditions and linguistic spaces open to more than one side, and saw translation as a vitalizing force in twentieth-century literature. 'An Indian English poet's Indianness', he said,

> is as questioned as are his claims to English. Most of his theoretical enemies argue that only a living Indian language can give a poet access to uniquely Indian experience.
>
> In the same vein they argue that since English is hardly a living Indian language, the Indian English poet's language is always dated or stilted or overstylized or is unnatural in other ways. These two major limitations stifle his self-expression from the outset and he has little freedom as an artist.
>
> These arguments are based on profound misconceptions about both the role of a native culture in literary art and the role of language in poetry. First, native cultures need not be considered

closed and static. In fact, closed and static cultures periodically die and become obsolete.

All surviving cultures in our increasingly shrinking global civilization have to create their own future in a global space and time. Nor is art the repetition of classic and therefore static information of a sacred kind. In fact, art generates new information within an open system which contains vast memory.

Literatures all over the world have become multi-traditional during the last few centuries. Linguistic spaces intersect one another, and where they fuse or split there are strange twilight areas. Since there is no country which speaks a poet's language, a poet's language itself becomes his landscape and his time . . .

When an Indian English poet writes, he can choose a British or an American idiom, or a neutral standard register as far as language is concerned, while his literary or stylistic tools could come from any Indian or foreign model even outside of English literature. The whole of world poetry in English translation could be his repertory. He can thus skip the concern for the surface structure of language and deal directly with the deeper structures and their relationship with poetic form. . . .

The potential strength of Indian English poetry is going to be derived from native Indian literatures and not without them. The ability to transform non-Anglo-Saxon cultural and poetic traditions into the global mainstream of English literature will give Indian English poetry its sustenance in the coming decades, provided Indian English poets—like the younger American poets, for example—discover the nourishing activity of poetic translation as a major aspect of creativity in the contemporary world.[1]

The title poem in *Travelling in a Cage* was written between 1975 and 1977, when Chitre lived in the United States, and, though its twenty-one mostly unpunctuated sections are in free verse, it employs several poetic and rhetorical devices: assonance and alliteration, refrain and parallelism, chiasmus and anaphora. Its epigraph, from Gray's *Anatomy*, is 'The heart is placed obliquely in the chest', and a sexual encounter, not always obliquely dealt with, seems to be at the heart of the sequence.

In a poem in which everything connects, and one cage leads to

[1] 'The Placelessness of Indian English Poetry', *Times of India* (Bombay), 6 May 1990, 13.

another, the reader can get confused not knowing which one he is in. Language (section 2) and sex (sections 5 and 7), with silence and sadness respectively—in one word, failure—built into them, are equally prisons, as is the sky. Just as Rimbaud associated vowels with colours, Chitre associates literary forms with modes of death:

> Murders are lyrics
> Genocide is epic
> But the greatest of all forms is suicide
> > (section 18)

Death, then, is a cage too, and only 'the greatest of all forms', self-murder, holds the key to freedom. The lines below are from the poem's last section:

> The quietness of an emptied vein
> Lies beyond manifestos and stars

In the other poems represented here, Chitre plays down his *De Profundis* side, employing a plainer, less inward-turning voice and a raconteur's tone. This can be deceptive, for in the last minute he is apt to cut the narrative ground of the poem from under the reader's feet. By the time 'The Felling of the Banyan Tree', 'Father Returning Home', and 'Panhala' end, Chitre has added a fourth dimension to each, pushing the poem into an area where its matter-of-fact opening seems small preparation.

The Light of Birds Breaks the Lunatic's Sleep

The light of birds breaks the lunatic's sleep
He wakes up moving out of a million dreams
His burning electric wires begin to glow
The lunatic's fingers extend like wires

Stretched out in the silence:
The lunatic's veins widen: he feels
Darkness roaring in place of blood:
That darkness is half a sleep: a wide

Awareness of a kind: even total sleep
Is a blaze in his brain: a flaming awareness
The lunatic watches a sound in the Sun:
And his eyes paraphrase the Sun:

Numberless sleeps and lightnings awaken
A vast lullaby in his flesh and blood
The lunatic sees a bird . . . flying . . . as his
eyelids flutter
And his eyes, drowning, begin to chirp.

from *Travelling in a Cage*

2

I came in the middle of my life to a
Furnished apartment. By now my pubic hair
Was already greying. And I could see the dirty

Old man under my own skin. It was not the
Absolute end but the beginning of it. The air
Smelt of dead rats and I was reaching the age of forty

In the manner one reaches an empty shelf. Where
Are all of you, my dear departed bald ones?
Angels wearing wigs, gods cleaning dentures?

106

I began to sit at the typewriter hurriedly hitting
Nails in the logs of silence. The ashtrays were full.
The tea grew cold before I remembered to drink it.

Words. More and more words. Clear as a city street
At midday. I will leave behind a more garbled version
Of the same world. The richer for my own noise.

And go. Often, in the middle of a poem, I would kill
Bugs and roaches with a powerful spray. A poem hardly
Upsets the balance of nature. O my effluents

Polluting the minds of others. The cancer of a lyric
Spreads through nameless lungs. I will teach you
Other ways of growing old, other ways of dying.

Through tunnels of light we reach out towards the darkness
From which we derive our common ink. In the middle of my life
I have come to a white page in which I must live.

5
The door I was afraid to open
Was autumn
One luminous month of remembering
Nothing
The dark smell of rotting leaves in her voice
While the sensuous shadows of trees burned in the river
I became an insect of solitude in the grass
Sitting at the very edge of the season

And in the yellow darkness of the bar
I inhaled another country's noise and perishable warmth
Looked in astonishment at her lips
Finely injured by a smile
And tried to guess the bitter taste of gin and tonic
As the rim of her glass shone directly in my eyes

Later we staggered home and undressed
Before I turned the light off I saw her skinny shoulders
What kind of wind was making love to leafless trees
Outside the door I was always afraid to open

7

All I hear is the fraying of the wind among splayed trees
The ailing voice of the sea in my mind's own distance
And her breasts shivering in the grey rain of my fingers
The skin has no memory and the memory no skin
How can I claim to have known the wetness of her mouth
A dog howled while we made love
And the window-pane was white as winter
Now that I have switched off the lights it is only a sheet
The smell of roasted meat still lingers in the room
And she is a sharp grain of salt to my unforgetting tongue
Tomorrow the hair of my poem will suddenly turn grey
The wind will have fallen when I enter
The sad space of the bathroom with its questioning mirrors

8

I woke up and looked at my empty white bed
Wondered if it looked slept in at all
I looked at the walls of my room and out the window
Wondered what the meaning of the word space was

I opened the faucets and watched the rushing miracle
Wondered what water really was and why it had to be wet
Then I looked into the mirror which was deep and clear
Wondered if the reverse of me was equally true

Then I opened a book of Ghalib's poems
In which he also wondered
What the cure of this disease was
What grass comes out of and what really is the air

19

Where can I hide now in this
Stark nakedness lit by a bare bulb
I have no country no continent to wear
Travelling without legs or language
Exposed and caged by my own condition
What doors can I open in this fear
What windows look out
And will I ever find my own face out there

Among monsters and children?

Inside the walls of this voice there are no bodies
Everything is as if cleaned out by a bomb
These long chains are only of words
Bearing the weight of no explanation

Will someone please at least tell me the name of my enemy?
And why these small flowers have this habit of clinging
To the barbed wire and growing all along it?

21

O quick knives curving into the core
And forests burning on the surface of water
Out of my eyes falls a planet
On which forgiveness grows

You have cut loose my song in a larger space
These bars of music are my last prison
The quietness of an emptied vein
Lies beyond manifestos and stars

I grow taller than all suffering
My feet touching the innocence of earth
My head beyond the gravity of gods
Touching the cloud of the saints

Spinning a deeper silence I vanish
At the edge of my own voice a world is ending

In Limbo

Dick Bakken came here driving his old van
Wearing the costume of the chicken of poetry
And Kazuko came all the way from Tokyo
Wearing the mask of a geisha
But still dark and swift as a suicidal samurai
Burt wore a black poncho and looked
Like a medieval adventurer his beard bristling
What scripts were we playing to
Am I going to have to play a Hindu
After all these years only because I happen to be
Here?
Poetry is the strangest form of incest
People making love to the same idea
With so many different bodies
And always feeling
Next to nothing as soon as they are done

Pushing a Cart

Pushing a cart through the brilliant
Interior of an American supermarket
It occurs to me that my private but hired refrigerator
Cannot contain all the hunger of India
What meats can I store in my mind
What fruits and cheeses can I hope to make permanent
These fat and insomniac mothers pushing their
Infants and groceries over these wide floors
Say nothing to a man temporarily exiled
Into affluence and freedom
Silently and not without envy
I warn the sexy undergraduate next to me
Watch your cholesterol, honey,
Who are you fattening yourself for, anyway?

DILIP CHITRE

Of Garlic and Such

Praise the garlic for its tight
Integration of cloves and its white
Concealment of unbearable astringence.

Praise the onion for keeping
Its eye-opening secret
Under so many identical skins.

Praise woman for her genderless
Passion hidden in a familiar body
The rippling enigma of her inner form.

Then damn yourself
Lord of nothing
Sheathe your murderous sword.

The Felling of the Banyan Tree

My father told the tenants to leave
Who lived in the houses surrounding our house on the hill
One by one the structures were demolished
Only our own house remained and the trees
Trees are sacred my grandmother used to say
Felling them is a crime but he massacred them all
The sheoga, the oudumber, the neem were all cut down
But the huge banyan tree stood like a problem
Whose roots lay deeper than all our lives
My father ordered it to be removed

The banyan tree was three times as tall as our house
Its trunk had a circumference of fifty feet
Its scraggly aerial roots fell to the ground
From thirty feet or more so first they cut the branches
Sawing them off for seven days and the heap was huge
Insects and birds began to leave the tree

III

9

And then they came to its massive trunk
Fifty men with axes chopped and chopped
The great tree revealed its rings of two hundred years
We watched in terror and fascination this slaughter
As a raw mythology revealed to us its age
Soon afterwards we left Baroda for Bombay
Where there are no trees except the one
Which grows and seethes in one's dreams, its aerial roots
Looking for ground to strike

Father Returning Home

My father travels on the late evening train
Standing among silent commuters in the yellow light
Suburbs slide past his unseeing eyes
His shirt and pants are soggy and his black raincoat
Stained with mud and his bag stuffed with books
Is falling apart. His eyes dimmed by age
Fade homeward through the humid monsoon night.
Now I can see him getting off the train
Like a word dropped from a long sentence.
He hurries across the length of the grey platform,
Crosses the railway line, enters the lane,
His chappals are sticky with mud, but he hurries onward.

Home again, I see him drinking weak tea,
Eating a stale chapati, reading a book.
He goes into the toilet to contemplate
Man's estrangement from a man-made world.
Coming out he trembles at the sink,
The cold water running over his brown hands,
A few droplets cling to the greying hairs on his wrists.
His sullen children have often refused to share
Jokes and secrets with him. He will now go to sleep
Listening to the static on the radio, dreaming
Of his ancestors and grandchildren, thinking
Of nomads entering a subcontinent through a narrow pass.

Panhala

The old fort has only one access.
From all other sides the mountain rises sheer.
Even the cliffs are almost faceless.

But this is about the elaborate garden
Inside the fort walls
The terraced rectangle to which stone steps lead down
And those very obscure trees
Whose leaves whisper sinister curses in the evening
They have a sort of light of their own
Neither black nor green
But as opaque as the silence
Even moonlight stays away from them
On such nights as the night of our visit
You thought only the wind and the headless horseman
Had the right to enter such a place.

Eunice de Souza

Eunice de Souza was born in Poona in 1940, and educated there and at Sophia College, Bombay. She received an M.A. from Marquette University, Wisconsin, in 1963 and a Ph.D. from the University of Bombay in 1988. She joined St Xavier's College, Bombay, in 1969 where she is now Lecturer in English. Apart from writing extensively on contemporary Indian culture and literature, she has written four books for children and is, with Adil Jussawalla, co-editor of *Statements* (1976), an anthology of Indian prose in English. Her collections of verse are *Fix* (1979), *Women in Dutch Painting* (1988), and *Ways of Belonging: New and Selected Poems* (1990), which was a Poetry Book Society Recommendation. She is represented in several recent anthologies of women's poetry, among them *Making for the Open: The Chatto Book of Post-Feminist Verse* (1984) and *Ain't I a Woman?* (1986).

Eunice de Souza's poems have the brevity, unexpectedness, and urgency of telegrams. In the first half of *Fix*, all the telegrams come from the Goan Catholic community to which she belongs. It is here that one meets, perhaps for the first time in Indian poetry, individuals whose English keeps the flavour of natural idiom without sounding picturesque or 'babu'. Francis X. D'Souza's incontestable line, 'these Hindu buggers got no ethics'; Phoebe asking if girls can get *'preggers* and all that, *when* / [they're] dancing' in 'Sweet Sixteen'; and Mrs Hermione Gonsalvez's 'In the good old days / I had looks *and* colour' are just three examples from as many poems of what her microphoned ear picks up at home, in church, at a party, and in the street.

I find these early poems as attractive today as when I first read them. With Goan names and its vernacular on her lips, Miss de Souza adopts the role of a community entertainer all right, but the performance, whatever else it may be, is of unsuspected value to *her*. The theatrical act, by giving her a grip on the rhythms of speech, releases the personal voice, her father, who died when she was still a child, central to it. ' "What have they done to my daddy?" ' she asks in one poem, and the crippling burden of 'For My Father, Dead Young' is 'I'm you.' Elsewhere she writes about herself in the same unflinching bare-fisted manner as she does about feeding the poor at

Christmas, though not, one should think, without an almost Larkin-esque self-irony:

> My enemies say I'm a critic because
> really I'm writhing with envy
> and anyway need to get married.
>
> my friends say I'm not
> entirely without talent.
>
> ('Autobiographical')

In a review, Adil Jussawalla describes the poems in *Fix* as bearing 'the stamp of today's terrible pain, endurance attempted now. On each page it blazons freshly. She makes no attempt to make us like or pity the persona and yet we find ourselves respecting it deeply. Those readers who prefer a softer or more lyrical line around its edge may find it extremely unpleasant.'[1] In 'One Man's Poetry', the last poem in the book, she says 'The rage is almost done'. And so it is.

Women in Dutch Painting is written by one who no longer 'heads for the abyss with / monotonous regularity'. The book's tone is more friendly than combative, and perhaps more resigned than friendly, but it has lost none of the dryness:

> That stare of perpetual surprise
> in those great green eyes
> will teach you
> to die alone.
>
> ('Advice to Women')

As the title of one poem puts it, these are 'Songs of Survival', and though she has not emerged unhurt—who could?—from the experiences in *Fix*, enough is saved for her to now advise and bless, travel and take notes, even wear, if half in jest, the old mask:

> I look striking in red and black
> and a necklace of skulls.
>
> ('For S. Who Wonders if I Get
Much Joy Out of Life')

---

[1]'One Woman's Poetry', *Journal of South Asian Literature*, 12, No. 1 (1983), 90.

Feeding the Poor at Christmas

Every Christmas we feed the poor.
We arrive an hour late: Poor dears,
like children waiting for a treat.
Bring your plates. Don't move.
Don't try turning up for more.
No. Even if you don't drink
you can't take your share
for your husband. Say thank you
and a rosary for us every evening.
No. Not a towel *and* a shirt,
even if they're old.
What's that you said?
You're a good man, Robert, yes.
beggars can't be, exactly.

Sweet Sixteen

Well, you can't say
they didn't try.
Mamas never mentioned menses.
A nun screamed: You vulgar girl
don't say brassières
say bracelets.
She pinned paper sleeves
onto her sleeveless dresses.
The preacher thundered:
Never go with a man alone
Never alone
and even if you're engaged
only passionless kisses.

At sixteen, Phoebe asked me:
Can it happen when you're in a dance hall
I mean, you know what,

getting *preggers* and all that, *when*
you're dancing?
I, sixteen, assured her
you could.

Miss Louise

She dreamt of descending
curving staircases
ivory fan aflutter
of children in sailor suits
and organza dresses
till the dream rotted her innards
but no one knew:
innards weren't permitted
in her time.

Shaking her greying ringlets:
'My girl, I can't even
go to Church you know
I unsettle the priests
so completely. Only yesterday
that handsome Fr. Hans was saying,
"Miss Louise, I feel an arrow
through my heart."
But no one will believe me
if I tell them. It's always
been the same. They'll say,
"Yes Louisa, we know, professors
loved you in your youth,
judges in your prime."'

Forgive Me, Mother

Forgive me, mother,
that I left you
a life-long widow
old, alone.

It was kill or die
and you got me anyway:
The blood congeals at lover's touch.
The guts dissolve in shit.

I was never young.
Now I'm old, alone.

In dreams
I hack you.

For My Father, Dead Young

I hold the child up in delight.
The revolving fan cuts her through.
It's a dream.
I'm you.
I heard your fumblings in the dark.
Woke on wet beds.
Kniving marshes.
I'm you.
You're the cold wind.
The grey mist.
The black dawn. The grinning skull.
I'm you.

de Souza Prabhu

No, I'm not going to
delve deep down and discover
I'm really de Souza Prabhu
even if Prabhu was no fool
and got the best of both worlds.
(Catholic Brahmin!
I can hear his fat chuckle still.)

No matter that
my name is Greek
my surname Portuguese
my language alien.

There are ways
of belonging.

I belong with the lame ducks.

I heard it said
my parents wanted a boy.
I've done my best to qualify.
I hid the bloodstains
on my clothes
and let my breasts sag.
Words the weapon
to crucify.

Women in Dutch Painting
(for Melanie Silgardo)

The afternoon sun is on their faces.
They are calm, not stupid,
pregnant, not bovine.
I know women like that
and not just in paintings—

an aunt who did not answer her husband back
not because she was plain
and Anna who writes poems
and hopes her avocado stones
will sprout in the kitchen.
Her voice is oatmeal and honey.

She and I

Perhaps he never died.
We've mourned him separately,
in silence,
she and I.

Suddenly, at seventy-eight,
she tells me his jokes,
his stories, the names of
paintings he loved,
and of some forgotten place
where blue flowers fell.

I am afraid
for her, for myself,
but can say nothing.

Eunice

Eunice, Embroidery Sister said
this petticoat you've cut
these seams
are worthy of an elephant
my dear

Silly braless bitch

Eunice is writing bad words sister
she's sewing up her head
for the third time sister

the limbs keep flopping
the sawdust keeps popping
out of the gaps
out of the gaps
out of the gaps
sister

Advice to Women

Keep cats
if you want to learn to cope with
the otherness of lovers.
Otherness is not always neglect—
Cats return to their litter trays
when they need to.
Don't cuss out of the window
at their enemies.
That stare of perpetual surprise
in those great green eyes
will teach you
to die alone.

For Rita's Daughter, Just Born

Luminous new leaf
May the sun rise gently
on your unfurling

in the courtyard always linger
the smell of earth after rain

the stone of these steps
stay cool and old

gods in the niches
old brass on the wall

never the shrill cry of kites

from *Five London Pieces*

III

MEETING POETS

Meeting poets I am disconcerted sometimes
by the colour of their socks
the suspicion of a wig
the wasp in the voice
and an air, sometimes, of dankness.

Best to meet in poems:
cool speckled shells
in which one hears
a sad but distant sea.

Adil Jussawalla

Adil Jehangir Jussawalla was born in Bombay in 1940 and educated at the Cathedral School there, and at University College, Oxford. After spending thirteen years in England, for four of which he taught at a language school in London, Jussawalla returned to India in 1970. Between 1972 and 1975 he was Lecturer in English at St Xavier's College, Bombay. He has published two volumes of poetry, *Land's End* (1972) and *Missing Person* (1976)—both unfortunately now hard to come by—and is the editor of *New Writing in India* (1974) and, with Eunice de Souza, *Statements* (1976), an anthology of Indian prose in English. Jussawalla has also written several important essays, dealing mainly with contemporary Indian culture. During the past fifteen years he has worked for various Bombay newspapers and magazines, and is at present literary editor of *Debonair*.

'In my own poems, mostly written abroad', Jussawalla says at the end of an essay on Indian poetry up to the mid-sixties, 'I have tried to show the effect of living in lands I can neither leave nor love nor properly belong to, and despite the occasional certitudes of poetry I am not at all sure where . . . my own . . . work . . . will lead.'[1] He is here referring to the poems in *Land's End*, at least some of which, for sheer musical complexity and the flow and counterflow of rhythm, are unequalled in the literature. Some two decades later, reiterating what he had said in the essay, Jussawalla told a critic, Bruce King, in an interview:

> In writing *Land's End* I did not have a conscious intention of writing poems only about being washed up. Now when I look at the poems, they seem to be about going astray, about a wasteland abroad, and about a resentment at being in England, not liking it there.[2]

What poets say about their work is seldom without interest; but their statements are one thing, and the poems, since they have an

[1] 'The New Poetry', in *Readings in Commonwealth Literature*, ed. William Walsh, Oxford, 1973, 89–90.
[2] 'An Interview with Adil Jussawalla', *The Indian Literary Review*, 4, No. 1 (January 1986), 4.

ADIL JUSSAWALLA

existence of their own, quite another. 'Land's End', 'Evening on a
Mountain' and 'Halt X', all taken from Jussawalla's first book, can
hardly be seen as expressions of 'resentment'. They are too strongly
affected by a sense of place for that. Though he may at times have
felt estranged from his surroundings, there are also occasions when
Jussawalla—whether standing at the south-western tip of England,
looking at a valley, or getting down at a wayside station in 'smudged
Derbyshire'—observed the landscape almost for its own sake, and
wrote what he observed:

> The valley sunned itself all day, its span
> Curving up two foothills . . .
>
> ('Evening on a Mountain')

> I counted sixty chimneys in a quarter
> The size of a burgher's courtyard . . .
>
> ('Halt X')

The feeling that undersets these poems does not interfere with the
traveller's sympathetic eye; on the contrary, it makes everything more
vivid:

> . . . far off,
> A cloud, launched from a rock, streaked
>
> North like a startled bird.
> ('Evening on a Mountain')

> A flock of pigeons dissolved in the viscid air
> Like a piece of mud in a current . . .
>
> ('Halt X')

Jussawalla wrote 'Land's End', surely the finest poem in the book,
when he was not yet twenty-two, at an age when the sensitive nerve is
most exposed, and rocks and seas feel like the body's extensions.
Indeed when you read it, his Hopkinsian lines rumble and crash with
something of nature's own 'brute power':

> Here in the cramped, pig's-footed county at last,
> Where seas grip, the airs kick and squall,
> Atlantic breakers boom, the sea-gull's fall
> Downwind to sheets of spray . . .

Running through the poem is the life-in-death impulse. One part of

124

nature, one creed, dies ('Rock Peter wavers; his planted footsteps fail') to vivify another part and a belief even more ancient:

> . . . though land sings
> Its consecrated rock, the sea sang earlier,
> To form the rock, to christen and to wreck.
> The sea renews itself as old rocks break.

Whereas 'Land's End' comes from experiencing in nature the forces that form, break and re-form, very different forces are at work further inland. Their effect is felt in the title sequence of Jussawalla's second book, *Missing Person*. A combination of factors—like the use of montage, discontinuous narrative, and, not least, the language that keeps shifting from the coarse to the elevated and back again—has given 'Missing Person' the reputation of being an uninviting text. 'While I try to break down defences', Jussawalla has himself said of it, 'I also build a few between the reader and the poem.'[3] Adding to the difficulty, *Missing Person* has been out of print for more than a decade.

The sequence consists of twenty-one poems in two parts; Part I, 'Scenes from the Life', has fourteen poems, and Part II, 'Points of View', seven. Jussawalla has explained how the two parts are related:

> In the first part I tried to get the feeling of a very quick-moving, rather jaggedly cut movie. I used popular elements—the clichétic line, the language of advertising. In some sense deliberately flat. In some of the individual poems, perhaps too much happens . . . Perhaps I tried to do too much . . . Of the second part I am more sure. These are individual poems with . . . the points of view of persons who have seen the not very edifying film of the missing person. The audience reaction.[4]

On the sequence as a whole, he says

> If there is any order in the sequence, it moves negatively; it is a regression. The sequence ends with a kind of tribal ripping apart of the missing person, who hardly exists anyway. All the cultures that have made him have made him invisible. The outside is stronger than he is . . . 'Missing Person' presents a problem, the guilt of the bourgeois intellectual. It does not get out of the problem. The uniqueness of the poem is in presenting the Indian bourgeois

[3] Quoted in *Two Decades of Indian Poetry: 1960–1980*, ed. Keki N. Daruwalla, New Delhi, 1980, 70.

[4] 'An Interview with Adil Jussawalla', 5–6.

intellectual, with links to other third world bourgeois intellectuals. I was trying to map the area. The poem doesn't offer any solutions.[5]

The sequence maps an area of historical rifts few Indian poets have looked at. The poets who precede Jussawalla, as those who come after him, either plunge down other—equally dangerous—gorges, or map a landscape whose topographical features are very different.

In Part II someone remarks of 'our two-bit hero', the missing person, 'His thoughts were bookish', and the sequence is in fact criss-crossed with literary references from nursery tales to Ezra Pound's *Hugh Selwyn Mauberley*, and with sound- and image-patterns. Reading it is like entering an echo-chamber that is sometimes also a hall of mirrors. Puns are words inside words, or mirrors inside mirrors, and the faint-hearted reader might decide to leave, as others will stay back to see what comes next, when Jussawalla, doubling the mirrored space in the auditorium, puns on 'reflect'. Here is the opening scene of 'Missing Person':

> House Full. It's a shocker. Keep still.
> Blood crawls from a crack.
> Keep still.
> It's all happening.
>
> It's a spear.
> It's your saviour.
> It's a quiet mirror with hair all over
>
> born
> to a middle-class mother.
> God's gift for further reflection.

'Once I was whole, I was all' Missing Person says as he watches a rerun of his fractured life, and then adds with a touch of hysteria, 'Believe, why don't you believe?' However, the unreacting mirror to which he is likened reflects only fragments, each fragment arranged, as in a cubist still-life, according to a different angle of vision.

So: in Part I, poem 3, the first fragment, 'A'. Set against it, an uncomprehending giggle, a schoolboy's titter, that extends to the third fragment, 'Osiris, Ra', tags from Egyptian mythology. The

[5] Ibid., 6–7.

fourth fragment, 'अ', pronounced 'er', is another first letter, but in the Hindi alphabet, and while the linguistic stew simmers in the post-colonial pot, the next fragment looks at language from a changed perspective. The अ, a splinter lodged among other splinters in Missing Person's cortical lobe, was 'once spoking your valleys with light.' Walter Benjamin would have characterized this view as 'historicism'. 'Historicism', he wrote, 'gives the "eternal" image of the past; historical materialism supplies a unique experience with the past', saying further that a historical materialist is someone who blasts open 'the continuum of history'. This is precisely what Jussawalla does next:

> But the a's here to stay.
> On it St. Pancras station,
> the Indian and African railways.
>
> That's why you learn it today.
>
> Look out the school at the garden:
> how the letter will happen
> the rest of your life:
> bright as a butterfly's wing
> or a piece of tin
> aimed at your throat . . .

Rhyme and assonance, the poet's tools, transform harmless insect wings into deadly projectiles, turn giggles into screams, and language into history. The poet, however, unlike the historian, can only blast it open at personal cost.

' "Get back to your language," they say', and little see what they have said, and in saying, hurled. But Jussawalla does, and it is time we listened to him.

Land's End

Here in the cramped, pig's-footed county at last,
Where seas grip, the airs kick and squall,
Atlantic breakers boom, the sea-gulls fall
Downwind to sheets of spray, the fast
Seas race, roil, slump and shower
Across the thrusted coastland; where brine-wings beat
The rooted perch of weeds and brine-grains bite
Raw rock or nerve exposed to their brute power,
Land's End or Faith's—what must I call
This faulted coast Atlantic breakers pound?
Wave after wave explodes, hour by hour
To undermine my numbed and bulwarked ground.

Cliff along cliff, the slack waves drag and hit
Their catch of sea-food against worn Land's End.
Lord, is this manna that you send
The startled tourists showered where they sit?
Black crabs splatter hard against the wall,
Scuttle to landed fish in crevices on cliffs:
Lord, your netted round of deep lifts
Its sweet fish to our lips; yet fishers haul
Against its tented pull; do you extend
Your power to your wan and sleeping Son,
Curled on a trawler troubled in that caul?
Will he walk your Tumult's first creation?

Rock Peter wavers; his planted footsteps fail;
The sea has fastened on; boats rock on springs;
His sloped arms gulp the bilge sea's spurning flings;
The funnel smoke is tattered like a veil.
Lord, *It is finished*: No man, beast or fowl
But needs a rock's assurance in this hour.
But neither sea nor Peter's praising tower
Holds Peter's weight; nor wind's howl.
No church stands on water: though land sings

Its consecrated rock, the sea sang earlier,
To form the rock, to christen and to wreck.
The sea renews itself as old rocks break.
Atlantic breakers pound our ended power.

Evening on a Mountain

The valley sunned itself all day, its span
Curving up two foothills; then the shadows
Crossed like wings across its back; further,

Ferries embroidered a slim lake, stitching
Silk into its cotton, prows snipping . . .
How still it was then! the sky thin and hollow,

Deflecting the words stoned across the valley,
The ears straining at each rebound; far off,
A cloud, launched from a rock, streaked

North like a startled bird.

Halt X

I

I do not know what station this is, or why
We broke our journey; checked, here in Derbyshire,
One senses danger, disquietude only.

Pieces of smoke litter the huddled town—
Card collage on felt; no pattering movement
On roads of sliding newspaper, sidling dog.
No alighting or descending the steps of its drizzling doors.

II

Rain fell like a drizzle of fine slag
On an anonymous town in smudged Derbyshire.
I counted sixty chimneys in a quarter
The size of a burgher's courtyard, wondered at smoke
Sliding edgeways through the dawn's widening slats.

A flock of pigeons dissolved in the viscid air
Like a piece of mud in a current; 5 o'clock.
A streetlamp craned its neck for the spreading frogs.

Bats

Shut in our jackets by the pale-green figs
We clung a branch and slept, till dawn exposed
The town and your grandmother praying; blind,
We sensed her shadow trembling on the twigs;
When she admonished Satan in her prayers.
We flew away to give her peace of mind.

Bats, bats you cried, and shutting up your ears
Scrambled for cover, while we dived and bombed
Peasants, beggars, rich fathers, richer sons.
We dropped like jackfruit by the hunters' guns,
Or tore like paper on your sizzling wires.
Manchild, remember what doctrinal fears
Flapped up when you saw not flying-fox
Nor dog nor mouse when hunting arms brought back
So many pink-tongued babies in a box.

ADIL JUSSAWALLA

from *Missing Person*

PART I

3

A———'s a giggle now
but on it Osiris, Ra.
An अ's an er . . . a cough,
once spoking your valleys with light.
But the a's here to stay.
On it St. Pancras station,
the Indian and African railways.

That's why you learn it today.

Look out the school at the garden:
how the letter will happen
the rest of your life:
bright as a butterfly's wing
or a piece of tin
aimed at your throat:

expansive as in 'air',
black as in 'dark',
thin as in 'scream'.
It will happen again and again—
in a library in Boston,
a death-cell in Patna.
And so with the other twenty-five letters
you try to master now—'cat', 'rat', 'mat'
swelling to 'Duty', 'Patience', 'Car'.

Curled in a cortical lobe (department of languages),
an unspeakable family gibbered.
'Where is their tape?' abroad, at a loss,
he asks. 'What does it say?'

'Wiped out,' they say.
'Turn left or right,
there's millions like you up here,
picking their way through refuse,

looking for words they lost.
You're your country's lost property
with no office to claim you back.
You're polluting our sounds. You're so rude.

'Get back to your language,' they say.

6

Black vamps break out of hell,
rave up a cold hotel,
never touch him.
White faggots fall at his feet,
fuck up his central heat,
never feel him.
He panics. His friends
leave him for their wives
as much part of living
as the carry-cots, the lifts.
Shut out of the warm and furry,
not wanted in Lucifer's halls,
a fire on one flat plane he drifts.

7

In a brief clearing
above an underworld of headless roots,
he sees a tree divide its parts
to bird, insect, sky,
locked to its reflection
by its wrist.

Exile's a broken axle.

Goes back (to where
whose travels cannot home?)

goes back to where

a mirror shakes in recognition.

9

He travels the way of devotion
but no sky lights
his street.

A river of pills brings him no raft.
Death goes awash with wishing.

Cripples his own mouth then, sits
killing his tongue, sits
barred up behind his teeth.

Bright sparks
on the international back-slapping circuit
are picking up prizes like static.

He's for the dark.

13

Less time for kicks
except for those
aimed at the face and balls.
Less time for pricks
who dig into his time.
He faints and falls.
Less time less time
to suffer liberation in the end,
to freeze one lovely frame
and hide there for a while.
The sockets jag. Time's disjointed all.
But left enough to bear
the last attempts at compromise
as student posters patch a crumbling wall
to hide the botched affair,
to smile and smile and smile.

PART II

1

No Satan
warmed in the electric coils of his creatures
or Gunga Din
will make him come before you.
To see an invisible man
or a missing person,
trust no Eng. Lit. That
puffs him up, narrows his eyes,
scratches his fangs. Caliban
is still not IT.
But faintly pencilled
behind a shirt,
a trendy jacket or tie,
if he catches your eye,
he'll come screaming at you like a jet—
savage of no
sensational paint,
fangs cancelled.

2

His hands were slavish;
but fingers burst out
from time to time
to point to a fresh rustling of tails
in the dustbin of history,
a new inflexion of sails
on the horizon.
His thoughts were bookish;
but a squall from the back of his skull
suddenly fluttered their pages,
making him lose his bearings,
abandon ship.

His cock, less rulable than his rest,
though fed on art-book types,
Hellenic forms,
plumped on libraries circulating
white bellies, white breasts,
with a catch in its throat,
jumped at nipples and arses
of indiscriminate races and classes.
His tongue,
his one underground worker perhaps,
bound by a sentence
pronounced in the West,
occasionally broke out
in a rash of yowls
defying the watch-towers of death,
police dogs:
a river of wild statistics;
or in riddles
crafted for cell-mates
aspiring to doctorates
from the Universities
of Texas, Bogota, Bombay,
perspiring
students of socio-linguistics.

5

Few either/ors
in underdeveloped lands,
mostly alsos:
the also-rans
the also-mad
the also-so-sos.

Renaissance Europe (our one-time twin)
was non-specialist also.
We're the mix
Marx never knew

would make the best
Communists. Also

too fond was our hero of distinctions,
too consistently separated torso from torso.
Where did that get the Greeks?
You see,
we're *Das Capital*, a dried-up well
and a big *Mein Kampf*. Also.

Nine Poems on Arrival

Spiders infest the sky.
They are palms, you say,
hung in a web of light.

Gingerly, thinking of concealed
springs and traps, I step off the plane,
expect take-off on landing.

Garlands beheading the body
and everyone dressed in white.
Who are we ghosts of?

You. You. You.
Shaking hands. And you.

Cold hands. Cold feet. I thought
the sun would be lower here
to wash my neck in.

Contact. We talk a language of beads
along well-established wires.
The beads slide, they open, they
devour each other.

Some were important.
Is that one,
as deep and dead as the horizon?

Upset like water
I dive for my favourite tree
which is no longer there
though they've let its roots remain.

Dry clods of earth
tighten their tiny faces
in an effort to cry. Back
where I was born,
I may yet observe my own birth.

Freedom Song

In '55 our sea-road kept a riot
of motorcycles going half the night.
Fresh out of school, we called it Freedom Road.
On Freedom Road no motherfucker's quiet.

No road block was *my* block. Full out, I felt
hot tits against my mouth, hot kisses, saw
blondes dancing in the dark, a cindertrack . . .
In '55 I knew I had to go.

In '66, a slow, round-shouldered man,
a quiet man, I came back to my street.
A cripple wheeled his wife by on a box
somewhere towards another Five-Year Plan.

Married and cool, now I don't attempt
jailbreaks and suicide, most of my evenings go
trying to get the guy out front and ask him
where in this land of Freedom's Freedom Road.

Connection

My father asks for mercy on the phone.
His voice is thin. I ask
who is it speaking? An old soldier
back for talks, thrusting a bandaged stump
against a door that hides a fat deserter.
I hold his last manuscript,
not having read a word this war-filled month.

Agha Shahid Ali

Agha Shahid Ali was born in Delhi in 1949 and grew up in Srinagar, Kashmir. He received an M.A. from the University of Delhi in 1970, and was in teaching before going to the United States in 1976. His subsequent degrees include a Ph.D. from the Pennsylvania State University (1984) and an M.F.A. from the University of Arizona (1985). He is now on the English faculty of Hamilton College, New York. The poems represented here are all from *The Half-Inch Himalayas* (1987), his first mature collection; previous to it he published *Bone-Sculpture* (1972) and *In Memory of Begum Akhtar* (1979). He is also the author of *T. S. Eliot as Editor* (1986) and *A Walk Through the Yellow Pages* (1987), a poetry chapbook. *The Rebel's Silhouette* (1991) consists of poems translated from the Urdu of Faiz Ahmed Faiz. A new collection of Ali's poems, *A Nostalgist's Map of America*, appeared in 1991.

Ali's poems seem to be whispered to himself, and to read them is as if to overhear. This is not to suggest that they are remote or in any way indistinct, but to underline the quietness of his voice and the clarity with which he speaks. A man talking to himself cannot afford to be strident, and, unless drunk, will choose each word with care:

> I always loved neatness. Now I hold
> the half-inch Himalayas in my hand.
>
> ('Postcard from Kashmir')

Though Ali has made exile his permanent condition, it is not what he writes about. Exile offers him unconfined and unpeopled space into which, one at a time, he introduces human figures. The eccentric and occasionally violent men of the family stand aloof from its women, who have the sensitivity of the well-born and from whom Ali inherits his own. Just as exile provides each memory with its own space, absence gives high definition to what is absent, be it landscape, lover, or self:

> When I return,
> the colours won't be so brilliant,
> the Jhelum's waters so clean,
> so ultramarine.
>
> ('Postcard from Kashmir')

139

The landlady says he lived here
for years. There's enough missing
for me to know him. On the empty shelves,
absent books gather dust: Neruda. Cavafy.

('The Previous Occupant')

Somewhere
without me
my life begins
('In the Mountains')

The language is always urbane, neutral, with individual lines and stanzas seldom calling attention to themselves. If anything, they tend to keep out of sight, making memorability a characteristic of the whole poem—each like a length of Dacca gauze—rather than of its separate parts.

Postcard from Kashmir

Kashmir shrinks into my mailbox;
my home a neat four by six inches.

I always loved neatness. Now I hold
the half-inch Himalayas in my hand.

This is home. And this the closest
I'll ever be to home. When I return,
the colours won't be so brilliant,
the Jhelum's waters so clean,
so ultramarine. My love
so overexposed.

And my memory will be a little
out of focus, in it
a giant negative, black
and white, still undeveloped.

(for Pavan Sahgal)

Snowmen

My ancestor, a man
of Himalayan snow,
came to Kashmir from Samarkand,
carrying a bag
of whale bones:
heirlooms from sea funerals.
His skeleton
carved from glaciers, his breath
arctic,
he froze women in his embrace.
His wife thawed into stony water,
her old age a clear
evaporation.

This heirloom,
his skeleton under my skin, passed
from son to grandson,
generations of snowmen on my back.
They tap every year on my window,
their voices hushed to ice.

No, they won't let me out of winter,
and I've promised myself,
even if I'm the last snowman,
that I'll ride into spring
on their melting shoulders.

Cracked Portraits

My grandfather's painted grandfather,
son of Ali, a strange physician
in embroidered robes, a white turban,
the Koran lying open on a table beside him.

I look for prayers
in his eyes, for inscriptions
in Arabic.
I find his will:
He's left us plots
in the family graveyard.

    ❁   ❁   ❁

Great-grandfather? A sahib in breeches.
He simply disappoints me,
his hands missing in the drawing-room photo
but firm as he whipped the horses
or the servants.

He wound the gramphone to a fury,
the needles grazing Malika Pukhraj's songs
as he, drunk, tore his shirts
and wept at the refrain,
'I still am young.'

❀   ❀   ❀

Grandfather, a handsome boy,
sauntered toward madness
into Srinagar's interior.
In a dim-lit shop he smoked hashish,
reciting verses of Sufi mystics.
My father went to bring him home.

As he grew older, he moved toward Plato,
mumbling 'philosopher-king',
Napoleon on his lips.
Sitting in the bedroom corner,
smoking his hookah, he told me
the Siberian snows
froze the French bones.

In his cup,
Socrates swirled.

❀   ❀   ❀

I turn the pages,
see my father holding a tennis racquet,
ready to score with women,
brilliance clinging to his shirt.

He brings me closer to myself
as he quotes Lenin's love of Beethoven,
but loses me as he turns to Gandhi.

Silverfish have eaten his boyhood face.

❀   ❀   ❀

143

Cobwebs cling
to the soundless
words of my ancestors.

No one now comes from Kandahar,
dear Ali, to pitch tents by the Jhelum,
under autumn maples,
and claim descent from the holy prophet.

Your portrait is desolate
in a creaking corridor.

(for Agha Zafar Ali)

The Dacca Gauzes

> ...for a whole year he sought
> to accumulate the most exquisite
> Dacca gauzes.
> —Oscar Wilde/*The Picture of
> Dorian Gray*

Those transparent Dacca gauzes
known as woven air, running
water, evening dew:

a dead art now, dead over
a hundred years. 'No one
now knows,' my grandmother says,

'what it was to wear
or touch that cloth.' She wore
it once, an heirloom sari from

her mother's dowry, proved
genuine when it was pulled, all
six yards, through a ring.

Years later when it tore,
many handkerchiefs embroidered
with gold-thread paisleys

were distributed among
the nieces and daughters-in-law.
Those too now lost.

In history we learned: the hands
of weavers were amputated,
the looms of Bengal silenced,

and the cotton shipped raw
by the British to England.
History of little use to her,

my grandmother just says
how the muslins of today
seem so coarse and that only

in autumn, should one wake up
at dawn to pray, can one
feel that same texture again.

One morning, she says, the air
was dew-starched: she pulled
it absently through her ring.

The Season of the Plains

In Kashmir, where the year
has four, clear seasons, my mother
spoke of her childhood

in the plains of Lucknow, and
of that season in itself,
the monsoon, when Krishna's

145

flute is heard on the shores
of the Jamuna. She played old records
of the Banaras thumri-singers,

Siddheshwari and Rasoolan, their
voices longing, when the clouds
gather, for that invisible

blue god. Separation
can't be borne when the rains
come: this every lyric says.

While children run out
into the alleys, soaking
their utter summer,

messages pass between lovers.
Heer and Ranjha and others
of legends, their love forbidden,

burned incense all night,
waiting for answers. My mother
hummed Heer's lament

but never told me if she
also burned sticks
of jasmine that, dying,

kept raising soft necks
of ash. I imagined
each neck leaning

on the humid air. She only
said: The monsoons never cross
the mountains into Kashmir.

The Previous Occupant

The landlady says he lived here
for years. There's enough missing
for me to know him. On the empty shelves,
absent books gather dust: Neruda. Cavafy.
I know he knew their poetry, by heart
the lines I love.

From a half-torn horoscope I learn
his sign: Aquarius, just like me.
A half-empty Flexsol in the cabinet:
he wore soft lenses. Yes, Aquarians are vain.
And no anthems on their lips, they travel
great distances. He came from some country
as far as Chile.

She says the apartment
will be cleaned by the 1st:

But no detergent will rub his voice from the air
though he has disappeared in some country
as far as Chile.
The stains of his thoughts still cling
in phrases to the frost on the windows.

And though he is blinded in some prison,
though he is dying in some country
as far as Chile,
no spray will get inside the mirror
from where his brown eyes,
brown, yes, brown,
stare as if for years he'd been
searching for me.

Now that he's found me,
my body casts his shadow everywhere.
He'll never, never, move out of here.

Vikram Seth

Vikram Seth was born in Calcutta in 1952 and educated at Doon School, Dehra Dun, and Tonbridge School in England. After taking his undergraduate degree—a first in politics, philosophy, and economics—at Corpus Christi College, Oxford, he went to Stanford University to work towards a Ph.D. on the economic demography of China. He has also studied at Nanjing University (China), and been a Wallace Stegner Fellow in Creative Writing at Stanford. He is the author of *From Heaven Lake* (1983), an award-winning travel book based on a hitch-hiking journey across Tibet; *The Golden Gate* (1986), a novel in verse, selected for the Sahitya Akademi Award of 1988; and three collections of poetry: *Mappings* (1981), *The Humble Administrator's Garden* (1985), which received the Commonwealth Poetry Prize for Asia, and *All You Who Sleep Tonight* (1990).

Perhaps Seth's teachers at Stanford have something to do with the way his poems are nicely poised between a tearful emotional state and its self-consciously dry-eyed, 'precisely hefted' verbalization. 'If I learned from Donald Davie', he says, expressing a debt acknowledged earlier, too, in the dedication of *Mappings*,

> that skill and form were not by themselves enough, what I learned from Timothy Steele was that passion and inspiration, by themselves, were not enough either. I learned this through work on my own poems, of course, but an equally effective lesson came from the work of other living poets who used form. Tim introduced me to the poetry of Philip Larkin whom again, ignorant economist that I was, I knew only as the compiler of *The Oxford Book of Twentieth Century English Verse*. But as I read Larkin (whose poem beginning 'The trees are coming into leaf / Like something almost being said', has a very similar formal shape to the very different poem that goes, 'They fuck you up, your mum and dad. / They may not mean to, but they do'), I began to realize the flexibility as well as the power and memorability of good 'formal' verse.[1]

Propelled by the nuts and bolts of his craft, someone reading Seth for the first time could easily miss the strong undertow of feeling.

[1] 'Forms and Inspirations', *London Review of Books*, 29 September 1988, 18.

'Ceasing Upon the Midnight' is written in rhyming tetrameter and trimeter couplets, the form of Marvell's 'Horatian Ode', but the flippant opening and the hypermetrical swing of the first two lines block out a slower note, struck in the second stanza, and culminating in the descending rhythms, with a distinct Coleridgean echo:

> ... anything
> But this meandering
>
> Down a dead river on a plain,
> Null, unhorizoned, whose terrain,
> Devoid of entity,
> Leads to no open sea.

Seth's manner, a parody of the grand romantic ode, while it hides the wound, 'The pus of memory', also, ultimately, reduces the pain: 'The bottle lies on the ground. / He sleeps. His sleep is sound'.

In 'The Humble Administrator's Garden', a conducted tour of visual clichés raises, in passing as it were, a never-to-be-settled moral issue: the price of making an artificial paradise. Beauty, Seth writes in a different context, 'I always am a sucker for'; and Mr Wang, a sucker himself where beauty is concerned, creates 'the loveliest of all gardens' through means dubiously acquired. Art is of such irreconcilables.

Seth's next book, *All You Who Sleep Tonight*, disappointed his many admirers. It has neither the innocence of *Mappings* nor the vigour and flourish of *The Humble Administrator's Garden*. The trouble with its poems is they give themselves up too quickly. Writing in the *Times of India*, Adil Jussawalla compared some of them to pop songs:

> The lines, easily remembered, easily rhymed, are equally easily forgotten, until they are heard again in other places, other contexts, recalling the first occasions they're associated with, which is what popular songs do.[2]

'Tradition is the soul of art' ends one such song in the book. More properly, it is the soul of craft, of verse-making, of certain skills that can be passed from father to son, or teacher to taught, and the two, the skills and the poem, should not be confused. In ten years, Seth's craft has flourished; the poetry has stayed where it was. Whereas he's

[2] 'Post-AIDS Lullabies', *Times of India*, 1 April 1990, 3.

added polish, refinement, and civility to his work, and given his language the sweetness of plain water, he has been unwilling to risk anything more than the simplest imaginative structures. The result this time is a poet's fitness exercises.

One exception, though, is 'Soon'. It's in the voice of a person dying of AIDS. The slowly uttered monosyllabic words, the limits imposed by the speaker's physical condition ('How am I to go on—'), the end-stopped lines, and the eye rhymes keep the poem's audibility to a minimum, making the reader come even closer to it. What he then hears is part love poem, part death-rattle. The whole is quite unforgettable.

Guest

I woke. He mumbled things in the next bed.
I lay there for an hour or so. At four
The alarm rang. He got out of bed. He wore
Nothing. I felt his sleepy classic head
And long-limbed body stir my quiescent heart.
I'd thought that I was free. Wrong from the start.
I found I loved him entirely instead.

There was no real hope. 'Guy loving guy?
Man—that's a weird trip—and not for me.'
I accepted that. But next day, warily,
We coiled to snap or spring. Rash truth. To lie
Still could have spared the trust; the warmth as well.
I left his room that day. I try to tell
Myself this sorrow like this ink will dry.

The Humble Administrator's Garden

A plump gold carp nudges a lily pad
And shakes the raindrops off like mercury,
And Mr Wang walks round. 'Not bad, not bad.'
He eyes the Fragrant Chamber dreamily.
He eyes the Rainbow Bridge. He may have got
The means by somewhat dubious means, but now
This is the loveliest of all gardens. What
Do scruples know of beauty anyhow?
The Humble Administrator admires a bee
Poised on a lotus, walks through the bamboo wood,
Strips half a dozen loquats off a tree
And looks about and sees that it is good.
    He leans against a willow with a dish
    And throws a dumpling to a passing fish.

Evening Wheat

Evening is the best time for wheat.
Toads croak.
Children ride buffaloes home for supper.
The last loads are shoulder-borne.
Squares light up
And the wheat sags with a late gold.
There on the other side of the raised path
Is the untransplanted emerald rice.
But it is the wheat I watch, the still dark gold
With maybe a pig that has strayed from the brigade
Enjoying a few soft ears.

The Accountant's House

We go in the evening to the accountant's house.
It is dark and the road is slush.
The fireflies fleck silver.
The ash flicked off by my companion, the barefoot doctor, is gold.

I want to clear up some questions on the income and expenditure
    account.
His wife and two daughters smile as I come in.
They pour tea. Their son died last Spring Festival.
We smile and discuss electricity fees.

This is my last day here. The Ministry of Education
Has decreed a two-and-a-half-week limit.
I will turn into a pumpkin soon enough
But today there is work, are pleasantries.

The green seedlings outside have been transplanted.
The accountant looks sad and my heart goes out.
No one knows how he died. He came home from play
And his head was hot, his nose bled, and he died.

Yet they laugh, yet they laugh, these lovely people,
And he clicks his abacus and she gives me a towel and the two
    girls
Smile shyly, boldly at the stranger and the father
Discussing matters of much importance together.

From an 'East is Red' Steamer

The old man in grey reproves the women's tears
And shouts from dock to deck. The sailor hears,
Smiles, flings a cigarette to a shorebound mate.
The Wuhan steamer hoots—two minutes late—
Plays martial music, exhorts us to do more
For the Four Modernisations, moves from shore,
While I the tourist view the mother and daughter
Waving across the broadening rift of water,
The grey and sunflecked water and the seagulls flying
Between the son and father, who now himself is crying.

Ceasing Upon the Midnight

He stacks the dishes on the table.
He wants to die, but is unable
    To decide when and how.
    Why not, he wonders, now?

A piece of gristle catches his eye.
The phone rings; he turns to reply.
    A smell of burning comes
    From somewhere. Something hums.

The fridge. He looks at it. This room
Would make an unpacific tomb.
    He walks outside. The breeze
    Blows warmly, and he sees

A sky brushed clean of dust and haze.
He wanders in a lucid daze
   Beneath the live-oak tree
   Whose creaks accompany

The drifting hub of yellow light
Low on the hillcrest. Ah, tonight,
   How rich it seems to be
   Alive unhappily.

'O sähst du, voller Mondenschein,
Zum letztenmal auf meine Pein',
   He murmurs to convince
   Himself its force will rinse

The pus of memory from his mind,
Dispel the dust he's swept behind
   The furniture of days,
   And with beneficent rays

Kindle the taut and tearless eyes
With the quick current of surprise,
   Joy, frenzy, anything
   But this meandering

Down a dead river on a plain,
Null, unhorizoned, whose terrain,
   Devoid of entity,
   Leads to no open sea.

The moon, himself, his shadow, wine
And Li Bai's poem may define
   A breath, an appetite,
   His link to earth tonight.

He gets a bottle, pours a glass,
A few red droplets on the grass,
   Libation to the god
   Of oak-trees and of mud,

Holds up its colour to the moon,
Drinks slowly, listens to the tune
    The branches improvise,
      Drinks, pours, drinks, pours, and lies

Face down on the moist grass and drinks
The dewdrops off its leaves. He thinks
    Of other moons he's seen
      And creatures he has been.

The breeze comforts him where he sprawls.
Raccoons' eyes shine. A grey owl calls.
    He imitates its cries,
      Chants shreds, invents replies.

The alcohol, his molecules,
The clear and intimate air, the rules
    Of metre, shield him from
      Himself. To cease upon

The midnight under the live-oak
Seems too derisory a joke.
    The bottle lies on the ground.
      He sleeps. His sleep is sound.

Unclaimed

To make love with a stranger is the best.
There is no riddle and there is no test.—

To lie and love, not aching to make sense
Of this night in the mesh of reference.

To touch, unclaimed by fear of imminent day,
And understand, as only strangers may.

To feel the beat of foreign heart to heart
Preferring neither to prolong nor part.

To rest within the unknown arms and know
That this is all there is; that this is so.

from *The Golden Gate*

7.1

When fear grows too intense to handle,
We shrink into a private smile,
Surprised when here and there a candle
Drives back the dark a little while,
A little space, before it gutters;
Or in the madness a voice utters
Words full of calm that to us seem
To bear the dry light of a dream
And stain our waking with more sorrow.
The night of hate that covers earth,
The generous country of our birth,
The single land from which we borrow
All that is ours—air, insight, tears,
Our fragile lives—for a few years,

7.2

That night of hate grows dense around us.
We laugh through what we can't dispel,
While apathy and terror hound us
On well-intentioned paths to hell.
Best to concede, to the septic chorus
Of the world's counsels, what's good for us,
And let them, if they choose to, mar
Our common earth with civil war.
Live day to day; relieve a little
What sorrow lies within our scope;
A moratorium on hope
Will, if it makes our laughter brittle,
Lend peace until that day of wrath
When the smooth doomtoys hurtle forth.

7·3

What, after all, is earth's creation?
A virus in the morgue of space.
What's Mozart but a weird vibration
Congenial to a brain-sick race
Rabid with virulence. Why bother
If things like these should maul each other
And, dying, yelp that they have won?
If clouds of dust occlude their sun
From them, it still shines undiminished
In its small galaxy. No change
Of note is likely when this strange
Irradiated beast has finished
Vomiting filth upon its bed
Of inhumanity, and is dead.

7·4

Some disagree. Heroic, silly
—Whichever—they have gathered here
In the pre-dawn, dew-damp and chilly,
On one of two days in the year
When light and night share day's dimension
In equal halves. To ease their tension
(For near them, where a cyclone fence
Delimits the circumference
Of Lungless Labs, police stand sentry,
Guarding a road, checkpost, and gate),
They sing aloud, and celebrate
Fall's sombre equinoctial entry
By lighting candles in an arc
Against the encroachment of the dark.

7·5

Dawn rises over Lungless redly.
The pioneers of the blockade
Are joined now by a motley medley;
A marching carnival parade

Starts out from Lungless Park, cavorting
Along to Lungless Labs, supporting
Those who risk prison to defy
The weaponry they all decry.
Young couples, schoolchildren, grandmothers,
Old hippies, punks with hair dyed green,
Staid-suited men who've never seen
Another demonstration, others
Who've been to scores, walk hand in hand
Toward the place where death is planned.

7.6

Those who devise these weapons—decent,
Adjusted, family-minded folk—
Don't think they plan death. Their most recent
Bomb (which, as an engaging joke,
They dubbed 'the cookie cutter') batters
Live cells and yet—this is what matters—
Leaves buildings and machines intact—
This butchering brainspawn is in fact
Soothingly styled a 'radiation
Enhancement device' by these same men.
Blind in their antiseptic den
To the obscene abomination
Of the refined ampoules of hate
Their ingenuity helps create,

7.7

They go to work, attend a meeting,
Write an equation, have a beer,
Hail colleagues with a cheerful greeting,
Are conscientious, sane, sincere,
Rational, able, and fastidious.
Through hardened casings no invidious
Tapeworm of doubt, no guilt, no qualm
Pierces to sabotage their calm.
When something's technically attractive,

You follow the conception through,
That's all. What if you leave a slew
Of living dead, of radioactive
'Collateral damage' in its wake?
It's just a job, for heaven's sake.

7.8

They breed their bombs here; others aim them
—Young targeteers at their controls—
At living souls, to kill and maim them
(Although their unemotive goals
Talk not of 'death' but 'optimizing
Effective yield'), while, mobilizing
Uncertain radar, we explore
The skies and prod ourselves to war.
Then, locked inside their lethal closet,
Go codes received, launch keys in place,
Bright crew-cut zombies will efface
All humankind. Too late to posit
What made them fire from the hip.
A flight of geese? A faulty chip?

7.9

Fatigues, down jackets, and bandannas,
Handicapped veterans in wheelchairs,
American flags and rainbow banners,
A band for Sousa, priests for prayers,
A replica of the grim reaper,
Placards—'I am my brother's keeper,'
'Nice folks don't use nukes,' 'Work for life,
Not death,' and a huge 'Strive with strife'—
Quarrelling, waving, wrangling, singing,
The lively ununanimous throng,
Two thousand minds, two thousand strong,
Submerge their disagreements, bringing
Common concern and hope to bear
Against the smithy of 'hardware'.

Soon

I shall die soon, I know.
This thing is in my blood.
It will not let me go.
It saps my cells for food.

It soaks my nights in sweat
And breaks my days in pain.
No hand or drug can treat
These limbs for love or gain.

Love was the strange first cause
That bred grief in its seed,
And gain knew its own laws—
To fix its place and breed.

He whom I love, thank God,
Won't speak of hope or cure.
It would not do me good.
He sees that I am sure.

He knows what I have read
And will not bring me lies.
He sees that I am dead.
I read it in his eyes.

How am I to go on—
How will I bear this taste,
My throat cased in white spawn—
These hands that shake and waste?

Stay by my steel ward bed
And hold me where I lie.
Love me when I am dead
And do not let me die.

Manohar Shetty

Manohar Shetty was born in Bombay in 1953, and educated at St Peter's High School, Panchgani, and the University of Bombay. Except for short periods between jobs, when he has worked in a restaurant and for a computer firm, Shetty has been a journalist since 1974. He now lives in Panjim, where he is editor of *Goa Today*. His stories have appeared in *Debonair* and *Indian Horizons*, and he has published two collections of verse, *A Guarded Space* (1981) and *Borrowed Time* (1988).

'Fireflies', the first poem in *A Guarded Space*, remembers a boyhood experience, the chase and capture of insects, but in the last stanza turns the trapped dying fireflies into a metaphor for adult life. The irony is that far from wanting to destroy their soft 'ornaments', the children provide them with food and air, and wish to save them. The poem indicates one of Shetty's obsessions. He often writes about being trapped, sometimes in the 'daily groove' of living, and sometimes in the 'grass-crammed bottle' of his own mind:

> Phantoms roaming in his head
> He wakes every morning from the spell of the dead.
> ('The Recluse')

> My mind is a gong;
> Something frayed inside
> Has to be replaced,
> The pressures stopped.
> ('Refrain')

The quotations are from different books, and both contain poems of malaise ('Slow as roots, soft as maggots'); boredom ('My bored mind invites things / I had shut out: the soft / Explosion of a runover pup'); and ennui (described as 'a whitish thing / Digging the crimson / Mud of his heart'). It is not unusual, then, for such a poet to be drawn towards enclosed or enclosing spaces (apartment kitchens, shop windows, cocoons, vaults, walls), and to detail the private amusements of lonely men:

> Two flat palms part
> and a bored crocodile yawns.
>
> ('Foreshadows')

Perhaps because he locks himself up thus, Shetty, on opening the eyes, finds the alphabet of seeing in a jumble. Everything still looks different even after he has straightened it out. He is especially good with animals, comparing bats to hung umbrellas and giant bowties, spiders to asterisks and yoyos (see 'Domestic Creatures' below), and ants—'magnified individually'—to puffed rice.

By writing about one thing at a time, he mostly stays clear of anthropomorphism. My preference, however, is for those of his poems that, while keeping the partition between inner weather and outer conditions intact, make it of transparent glass:

> It was there when I started off:
> Pale as a woodshaving, glued
> To windowglass, unmoved by
> Thumps of bags, the slamming
> Of doors, the cheerless goodbyes.
>
> ('Departures')

For the rest of the sixteen-hour journey Shetty is glued to the moth, and without once transgressing its space—its 'one square inch'—makes it also his own.

Fireflies

Outside, they were flashing streamers.
But straying indoors like wavering lanterns
Into widening shadows thrown by excited
Nets of caps and blazers, we caged them
In grass-crammed bottles, the tops
Punctured for air, and watched them
Stare like luminous dials.

I had imagined burning crystals
Or tips of emerald embers,
But found a softer substance—
Soon dimming—the insects, worried
By coarse hands, the walls of glass
Baffling their tiny wings,
Wilted to lifeless specks.

I had felt nothing then.
Only a small pang for the loss
Of a schoolboy's ornament. But now,
Travelling my daily groove
In the hunt for food and habitat
I remember their trapped blank lights.

Foreshadows

Waiting for the shy click of heels
on the stairs, I watch a deep
forest rise from my hand:
On the green glowing wall
my looped thumb and fingers
transfer a pensive fawn
Two flat palms part
and a bored crocodile yawns
Wild cats roll and purr
when my fingers convert to ears

Giant butterflies dip and disappear
as the door-bell rings like a shrill bird.
A faint smell of musk enters
as I lope across the wall
My mouth exposes hungry tusks
and hands reach out like paws . . .

Gifts

You unfold, like starfish,
On a beach, your touch
Stills the rumpled sea,
Hair, plastered sea-weed.

I come from the labyrinths:
Traffic lights park in my eyes
Before I cross, highways fork and
Stream like veins in my hand.

You hunger for a blade of grass
In the welter of concrete,
I step on softening sand
Suspiciously. Together

We trace a bridge: you pick
A shell translucent as neon,
And I a tribal earring
Reflected in plate glass.

Wounds

For a year it was its home,
The sill and window behind
My bed, and each night I saw
The scattered grain had gone.

The guarded eyes, the torn wing
Like a neglected hedge,
Fluttered in greeting; then it
Flapped up to sleep, rocking
Precariously, as on a trapeze.

It became something of a friend
With its rhythmic murmuring.
Sometimes, tilting off
The window's edge, its dribbling
Descents intruded on my
Avian dreams: birds perched
On my shoulders, birds
Feeding out of my hand, and
Skirring about in a cloud.

But that one night a livid
Flash broke through my head;
Five times it reeled over
As from a cliff, its wounded wing
Thrashing down the window,
Spilling squalls of feathers
On my pillow, uprooting me
From the tense moorings of sleep.

I remember the startled eye,
The pulsing, iridescent breast,
As it flinched from the sharp slap,
And fell off the sill.
I remember it swerving, rising
Clumsily on its one good wing
To teeter on a roof's rim,
Then drop like a stone.

I dreamt, then, of lame dogs,
Abattoirs, and pulped frogs.
Now several nights have passed,
And I have no dreams at all.

Domestic Creatures

LIZARD

Tense, wizened,
Wrinkled neck twisting,
She clears
The air of small
Aberrations
With a snapping tongue,
A long tongue.

PIGEON

Swaddled cosily, he
Settles by the window,
Burping softly;
Eyelids half-closed,
Head sinking
In a fluffy
Embroidered pillow.

SPIDER

The swollen-headed spider
Spins yarns from her corner.
Tenuous threads of her tales
Glitter like rays
From the fingertips of a saint.

She weaves on, plays along,
Hangs from a hoary strand,
Rolls, unrolls: a yoyo,
A jiggling asterisk: a footnote:
Little characters transfixed
In the clutches of her folds.

COCKROACH

Open the lid, he tumbles out
Like a family secret;

166

Scuttles back into darkness;
Reappears, feelers like
Miniature periscopes,
Questioning the air;
Leaves tell-tale traces:
Wings flaky as withered
Onion skin, fresh
Specks scurrying
In old crevices.

Bats

After dark, no longer hung umbrellas,
Black bull's-eyes, or wrapped
Shut as catatonics, they swept
Through moon-gilded windows,
Gliding across the walls
Like giant bow-ties; over heads
Sleeping in neat rows,
Dreaming of creaking capes,
Catacombs, crimson teeth
Dipping into sweet veins.

Awakened by the whooshing shadows,
Blood rising at their inverted lives,
With towels and blazers we slapped
Them to the cold floor: they flapped,
Toes twitching, the rowing tracery
Of wings grounded, huddled,
Pouting foxfaces startled
By the stark lights. Later, we heard
Of their soundless cries.

Departures

It was there when I started off:
Pale as a woodshaving, glued
To windowglass, unmoved by
Thumps of bags, the slamming
Of doors, the cheerless goodbyes.

I forgot it for an hour:
The black and white milestones
A fleeting clockface ticking
The distance away from
What had once been home.

The road was dragged back,
A measuring tape; dark
As an eel it unreeled
Glistening and writhing on land.
The bus heaved

On the tangent bends.
The moth was still, like
Something embossed.
Mindless refugee, would it
Whisper sensible secrets to me?

Wrapped in peace, its wings
A neat canvas tent, distance
Never came to an end; live
Minuscule mummy in a pyramid
Of sky, trees and fertile air!

Midnight halt in a strange town:
Lurid yellow glare of stalls,
Odd brand names, a southern
Tongue which slithered
Like snakes in a glass case.

I made uneasy small talk:
Hotel rates, places of interest,
Rents, the distance left.
A few replied with a sleepy air.
Some didn't know, or care.

Back for the last leg—
The stowaway motionless
As a pinned specimen, at home
On a transparent bed of glass.
Was it asleep or dead?

For sixteen hours it had stuck
To one square inch of space!
Blind to my destination, glimpsed
Coruscating from a high bridge;
The waters below a whirling sheet

Pulled out from under my feet;
I felt like a stone
Tensing in the air—hanging fast
To my light exemplar
Still rooted to glass.

Moving Out

After the packing the leavetaking.
The rooms were hollow cartons.
The gecko listened stilly—
An old custom—for the heartbeat
Of the family clock.

After the springcleanings
Now the drawing of curtains.
I thought of the years between
These grey walls, these walls
Which are more than tympanic.

169

There remained much, dead and living,
Uncleared, unchecked; dust mottled
Into shreds under loaded bookshelves;
The fine twine of a cobweb
Shone in the veranda sunlight.

All this I brushed aside along
With the silverfish in flaking tomes,
The stains on marble and tile
Scoured with acid; but the ghosts
Loomed like windstruck drapes;

Like the rectangle left by
A picture frame: below a nail
Hooked into a questionmark,
A faint corona,
A contrasting shade.

Select Bibliography

Alexander, Meena. 'Jayanta Mahapatra: A Poetry of Decreation', *Journal of Commonwealth Literature*, 18, No. 1, 1983.

Amirthanayagam, Guy. 'Kolatkar's *Jejuri*: A Pilgrimage into the Past and the Present', *Only Connect: Literary Perspectives East and West*, ed. Guy Amirthanayagam and S. C. Harrex. Adelaide: Centre for Research in the New Literatures in English, 1981.

Amur, G. S. 'The Poetry of Exile: An Introduction to Adil Jussawalla', *Indian Poetry in English: A Critical Assessment*, ed. Vasant A. Shahane and M. Sivaramakrishna. Delhi: Macmillan, 1980.

Bhabha, Homi. 'Indo-Anglian Attitudes', *Times Literary Supplement*, 3 February 1978.

Bhabha, Homi. 'Interrogating Identity. The Real Me: Post-Modernism and the Question of Identity', ICA Documents 6. London: Institute of Contemporary Arts, 1988.

Chitre, Dilip, ed. *An Anthology of Marathi Poetry: 1945–1965*. Bombay: Nirmala Sadanand, 1967.

Chitre, Dilip. 'Poetry in the Enemy's Tongue: On Two Indian Poets Writing in English' (Adil Jussawalla, Jayanta Mahapatra), *New Quest* (Pune), No. 14, March–April 1979.

Chitre, Dilip. 'Life on the Bridge', *Bombay Literary Review*, No. 1, 1989.

Chitre, Dilip. 'The Placelessness of Indian English Poetry', *Times of India* (Bombay), 6 May 1990.

Daruwalla, Keki N., ed. *Two Decades of Indian Poetry: 1960–1980*. Delhi: Vikas Publishing House, 1980.

Daruwalla, Keki N. 'Drawing on History', *Keynote* (Bombay), No. 2, April 1982.

Daruwalla, Keki N. 'National Identity and Indian Poetry in English', *Indian Horizons* (New Delhi), 32, No. 4, 1983.

Engblom, Philip C. 'Modernisms in Bombay: Marathi and English Versions', *Bombay Literary Review*, No. 1, 1990.

Ezekiel, Nissim. 'Two Poets: A. K. Ramanujan and Keki N. Daruwalla', *Illustrated Weekly of India*, 18 June 1972.

Ezekiel, Nissim. *Selected Prose*. Delhi: Oxford University Press, 1992.

Haq, Kaiser, ed. *Contemporary Indian Poetry*. Columbus, Ohio: Ohio State University Press, 1990.

Harrex, S. C. 'A Critical Approach to Indo-English Poetry', *Only Connect: Literary Perspectives East and West*, ed. Guy Amirthanayagam and S. C. Harrex. Adelaide: Centre for Research in the New Literatures in English, 1981.

Jussawalla, Adil. 'The New Poetry', *Readings in Commonwealth Literature*, ed. William Walsh. Oxford: Clarendon Press, 1973.

Jussawalla, Adil. 'The New India, The New Media and Literature', *The Indian Pen* (Bombay), Nos. 1–2, January–February 1985.

Jussawalla, Adil. 'Kill that Nonsense Term', *Debonair* (Bombay), May 1988.

Jussawalla, Adil. 'Being There: Aspects of an Indian Crisis', *Bombay Literary Review*, No. 1, 1989.

Karnani, Chetan. *Nissim Ezekiel*. New Delhi: Arnold-Heinemann, 1974.

Kher, Inder Nath, guest ed. *Journal of South Asian Literature* (East Lansing, Michigan), 11, Nos. 3–4, Spring–Summer 1976 [Nissim Ezekiel issue].

Kimbahune, R. S. 'From *Jejuri* to Arun Kolatkar', *New Quest* (Pune), No. 19, January–February 1980.

King, Bruce. 'Modern Indian and American Poetry: Some Contacts and Relations', *Indian Journal of American Studies* (Hyderabad), 15, No. 1, Winter 1985.

King, Bruce. 'An Interview with Adil Jussawalla', *Indian Literary Review* (New Delhi), 4, No. 1, January 1986.

King, Bruce. *Modern Indian Poetry in English*. Delhi: Oxford University Press, 1987.

King, Bruce. *Three Indian Poets* (Nissim Ezekiel, A. K. Ramanujan, Dom Moraes). Madras: Oxford University Press, 1991.

Kulshrestha, Chirantan. 'The Self in A. K. Ramanujan's Poetry', *Contemporary Indian English Verse: An Evaluation*, ed. Chirantan Kulshrestha. New Delhi: Arnold-Heinemann, 1980.

Lall, E. N. *The Poetry of Encounter: Dom Moraes, A. K. Ramanujan and Nissim Ezekiel*. New Delhi: Sterling, 1983.

Mahapatra, Jayanta. 'The Inaudible Resonance in English Poetry in India', *The Literary Criterion* (Mysore), 15, No. 1, 1980.

Mahapatra, Jayanta. 'About "Hunger" and Myself', *Keynote* (Bombay), No. 1, March 1982.

Mahapatra, Jayanta. 'The Stranger Within: Coming to Terms through Poetry', *Dalhousie Review*, 63, No. 3, 1983.

Mahapatra, Jayanta. Autobiographical essay in *Contemporary Authors*, Autobiography Series, 9, series ed. Mark Zadrozny. Detroit, Michigan: Gale Research Company, 1989.

Mehrotra, Arvind Krishna. 'The Emperor Has No Clothes', *Chandra-bhāgā* (Cuttack), No. 3, Summer 1980 and No. 7, Summer 1982.

Moraes, Dom. *My Son's Father: An Autobiography*. 1968; rpt. New Delhi: Penguin Books, 1990.

Moraes, Dom. 'Time and the Poet', *Debonair* (Bombay), October 1989.

Moraes, Dom. 'Prose Thoughts on Verse', *Debonair* (Bombay), April 1990.

Nabar, Vrinda. 'Keki N. Daruwalla: Poetry and a National Culture', *Indian Poetry in English: A Critical Assessment*, ed. Vasant A. Shahane and M. Sivaramakrishna. Delhi: Macmillan, 1980.

Naik, M. K. *A History of Indian English Literature*. New Delhi: Sahitya Akademi, 1982.

Nazareth, Peter. 'Adil Jussawalla Interviewed', *Vāgartha* (New Delhi), No. 25, July 1979.

Padhi, Bibhu Prasad. 'The Parallel Voice: A Study of the New English Poetry in India', *Quest* (Bombay), No. 98, November–December 1975.

Paniker, K. Ayyappa. 'The Poetry of Jayanta Mahapatra', *Indian Poetry in English: A Critical Assessment*, ed. Vasant A. Shahane and M. Sivaramakrishna. Delhi: Macmillan, 1980.

Parthasarathy, R., ed. *Ten Twentieth-Century Indian Poets*. Delhi: Oxford University Press, 1976.

Parthasarathy, R. 'How It Strikes a Contemporary: The Poetry of A. K. Ramanujan', *The Literary Criterion* (Mysore), 12, Nos. 2–3, 1976.

Patel, Gieve. 'Daruwalla's Asoka Poem and Patwardhan's Draw-ings in Time', *Contemporary India: Essays on the Uses of Tradition*, ed. Carla Borden. New Delhi: Oxford University Press, 1989.

Peeradina, Saleem, ed. *Contemporary Indian Poetry in English: An Assessment and Selection*. Bombay: Macmillan, 1972.

Perry, John Oliver. 'Neither Alien nor Postmodern: Jayanta Maha-patra's Poetry from India', *Kenyon Review*, 8, No. 4, Fall 1986.

Perry, John Oliver. 'Finding an Appropriate Multicultural Pers-pective for Indian English Poetry', *Bombay Literary Review*, No. 2, 1989.

Ramanujan, A. K. 'Classics Lost and Found', *Contemporary India: Essays on the Uses of Tradition*, ed. Carla Borden. New Delhi: Oxford University Press, 1989.

Sarang, Vilas, ed. *Indian English Poetry since 1950: An Anthology*. Bombay: Disha Books, 1990.

Seth, Vikram. 'Forms and Inspirations', *London Review of Books*, 29 September 1988.

Singh, Amritjit, *et al. Indian Literature in English: 1827–1979*. Detroit, Michigan: Gale Research Company, 1981.

Singh, Brijraj. 'Four New Voices' (Arvind Krishna Mehrotra, Arun Kolatkar, Gieve Patel, Adil Jussawalla), *Chandrabhāgā* (Cuttack), No. 1, 1979.

Sivaramakrishna, M. 'The "Tongue in English Chains": Indo-English Poetry Today', *Indian Poetry in English: A Critical Assessment*, ed. Vasant A. Shahane and M. Sivaramakrisha. Delhi: Macmillan, 1980.

Vinson, James and D. L. Kirkpatrick, eds. *Contemporary Poets*, 4th edition. London: St. James Press, 1985.

Walsh, William. *Indian Literature in English*. Longman Literature in English Series. London and New York: Longman, 1990.

Index of Titles

175

13

Index of First Lines